P9-CRE-614

KNOW
FEAR

KNOW FEAR

FACING LIFE'S
SIX MOST COMMON PHOBIAS

ED YOUNG, JR.

BROADMAN
&HOLMAN
PUBLISHERS

NASHVILLE, TENNESSEE

© 2003 Ed Young, Jr.
All rights reserved
Printed in the United States of America

0-8054-2572-1

Published by Broadman & Holman Publishers
Nashville, Tennessee

Dewey Decimal Classification:152.4
Subject Heading:FEAR \ PHOBIAS

All Scripture quotations, unless otherwise noted, are taken from The Holy Bible, New International Version (North American Edition), copyright © 1973, 1978, 1984 by the International Bible Society. Used by permission of Zondervan Publishing House. Scripture quotations marked (NLT) are taken from the Holy Bible, New Living Translation, copyright © 1996. Used by permission of Tyndale House Publishers, Inc., Wheaton, Illinois 60189. All rights reserved. Scripture quotations marked (NKJV) are taken from the New King James Version, copyright © 1979, 1980, 1982. Used by permission of Thomas Nelson, Inc., Nashville, Tennessee. All rights reserved. Scripture quotations marked (NASB) are taken from the New American Standard Bible, copyright © The Lockman Foundation 1960, 1962, 1963, 1968, 1971, 1973, 1975, 1977. Used by permission. Scripture quotations marked (TLB) are taken from The Living Bible, copyright © 1971. Used by permission of Tyndale House Publishers, Inc., Wheaton, Illinois 60189. All rights reserved. Any emphases or parenthetical comments within Scripture are the author's own.

Written permission must be secured by the author to use or reproduce any part of this book, except for occasional page copying for personal study or brief quotations in critical reviews or articles.

1 2 3 4 5 6 7 07 06 05 04 03

CONTENTS

ACKNOWLEDGMENTS

This book has been in the works for quite some time, and it is difficult to thank everyone who has been involved in the process from start to finish. But I do want to acknowledge several people on my staff who have helped immensely in getting this manuscript published.

To Cliff McNeely, who has driven this project over the past two years, thanks for initially contacting the publisher with the book proposal, and for your invaluable help with research, writing, and editing. I literally could not have completed this book without your perseverance and dedication to the project.

To Jessica Lonsdale, who assisted Cliff at the beginning of the project, thank you for getting us started on the book proposal and for your good work in editing and research.

And to Lynn Cross, I owe many thanks for her years of work and dedication in transcribing many of my sermon series' transcripts, one of those series being the basis for this book.

And, as always, much gratitude goes out to the people of Fellowship who give me the great thrill of opening up God's Word to them week in and week out. Thanks for your commitment to Fellowship Church and the incredible difference you make for Christ in our community and the world.

INTRODUCTION

Getting a Grip on Fear

It was a time of great uncertainty. Many people warned of social and cultural upheaval, of hardship, famine, and trouble. Others worried about the coming of the end of the world. Prophecies abounded about the return of Christ, as religious numerologists predicted the year of his return from various apocalyptic formulas and codes. Reports and rumors spread of troubling signs and wonders around the world. Countries and governments, communities, families, and individuals were poised for the approaching millennium.

With the recent turning of the millennial clock fresh on our minds, all of the fear-mongering I have just described sounds pretty familiar. Doesn't it? Well, hold on to your Y2K party hats, because these descriptors are not about the time leading up to the recent millennial changeover but the one before it. That's right. Boston's Center for Millennial Studies has gathered vast amounts of research indicating that many of the same rumors, worries, and predictions we experienced in Y2K were prevalent one thousand years ago, in Y1K.[1] The psychological and spiritual state of mankind was not much different in the years leading up to the coming of the second millennium than it was for us in the past few years leading up to the third. The main difference, of course, is that news and rumors did not travel quite so fast back in the years preceding A.D. 1000.

However, in our modern technological age with information traveling at the speed of light around the world and back, a kind of global panic set in as many of us trembled in our newly purchased combat boots waiting for our computers, cell phones, and Palm Pilots to blow up at the stroke of midnight on January 1, 2000. Some people thought that terrorists would strike, the stock market would crash, and the power would go out. Some of us bought emergency supplies of bottled water and batteries. And the sales of dry food survival packs and gas-powered generators were staggering. Some people even dug shelters and liquidated their financial portfolios. As everyone hunkered down, the mantra of the day was, "Are you Y2K OK?" Are you Y2K compliant?

As you may have already realized, this whole process revolved around fear: fear of the unknown. I think it's safe to say, in retrospect, that Y2K can be labeled "the year of fear." The ever-rising hoopla caused a lot of us to freak out. But, needless to say and to the surprise of many, we have managed to survive the turning of the millennium and beyond.

Nonetheless, the whole Y2K process underscores the reality that the world today is paralyzed by fear. Everywhere we turn we seem to find another thing to add to our growing list of phobias, fears, and anxieties. We even have extensive lists categorizing all of these modern-day phobias. There are more fears out there than you have probably ever thought possible—some of them odder than others. Allow me to list just a few examples of the bizarre things that we humans fear:[2]

- Arachnophobia is the fear of spiders.
- Aerophobia is the fear of flying.
- Claustrophobia is the fear of confined spaces.
- Dentophobia is the fear of dentists.
- Glossophobia is the fear of speaking in public.
- Hamartophobia is the fear of sinning.
- Liaphobia is the fear of lying—just kidding; I made that one up.
- Pentheraphobia is the fear of your mother-in-law.
- Ecclesiophobia is the fear of church (especially at a 10:05 kickoff time, right?).
- Ternophobia is the fear of being tickled by feathers.
- Venustraphobia is the fear of beautiful women.
- Xanthophobia is the fear of the color yellow.
- Anuptaphobia is the fear of staying single.
- Blennophobia is the fear of slime. (I've got to say that I am not very keen on slime.)
- Gamophobia is the fear of marriage.

You won't believe this one:

- Luposlipaphobia is the fear of being pursued by timber wolves around a kitchen table while wearing socks on a freshly waxed floor. (I did not make that up.)

Fear is a fascinating subject and not just because some fears are humorous. Fear is fascinating because it has two sides. There is a negative side to fear in that it can paralyze us and tyrannize our lives.

It can keep us from being all that God wants us to be. But fear also has a positive side. Fear is able to stimulate and motivate us to greatness. It can drive us to do the things we know God wants us to do with the life he has given us.

What I am about to say may surprise you, but many people claim that they do not have to deal with fear at all. They say, "Well, I am autonomous. I am self-sufficient. I don't deal with fear because I can handle anything that comes my way." If you say that, watch out, because your fears are going to surface like a submarine under a depth-charge attack. Chances are you are living with deep-seated fear that you have not understood, processed, or dealt with.

In this book, fear is dealt with in two broad categories. The first category deals with the many common fears that we all face in this life—the fear of helplessness, the fear of the future, the fear of commitment, the fear of failure, the fear of loneliness, and the fear of death. All of these fears have an aspect of uncertainty to them. We fear most that which is unknown to us.

The second category of fear is handled in the last several chapters. These chapters address a healthy kind of fear—the fear of God. As we move from unfounded fears to this radically different type of fear, the antidote to earthly fear will become evident in the eternal character of a loving but just heavenly Father.

The Bible is not silent on the subject of fear. Second Timothy 1:7 says, "For God has not given us a spirit of fear, but of power and of love and of a sound mind" (NKJV). That word *fear* in this passage comes from the Greek term *phobas,* which means "cowardice, timidity, running scared." This is the only place in the New Testament where *phobas* is used.

The spirit of God does not produce negative fear; rather, it produces love and power and a sound mind. Your Bible translation might refer to a sound mind as "self-discipline." God knew that we would deal with and process a lot of fear. That is why the phrase "fear not" is mentioned 189 times in the Bible. Many Christians know that fear and anxiety show a lack of faith in God, but what they do not know is how to deal with that fear. Instead they are left feeling afraid, guilty, and helpless.

I need to make a very sobering statement at this point. As you read this book right now, you may have every reason to live in fear. You know that to continue with the low-grade level of commitment in your marriage, it will just be a matter of time before attorneys are called in to pick up the pieces. You know that if you continue with the current level of integrity in your friendships and business relationships, the future will not be quite so bright.

Maybe you know that if you remain in your cocoon of comfort—not taking risks, not stepping out, and afraid of failure—your life will be riddled with regret. You know that God wants you to accomplish so much more in your life, but you just don't know how to break through the cycle of fear that keeps you from experiencing success in life.

You may be plagued with a fear of the greatest of life's unknowns—the future. You look ahead in your life and that of your family's, and you freeze up from the fear in your heart. All of the variables that are beyond your control at every turn in the bend send you running to hide under the bed. How can you possibly plan for every eventuality you may be required to face? Is there any way to find a sense of peace and contentment about all of the unknowns in your future?

Maybe you are fearful of being alone. As you stare at the radar screen of your relational world, it doesn't look very promising. You are single and desperately want the wedding ring and the white picket fence, along with the beautiful little house and the 2.3 children, but at this point things are not going your way. Maybe you are getting older, thinking about living alone, and the fear of being all by yourself in this world is paralyzing. You don't have anyone who really understands you or knows you or, you think, who loves you.

All of these anxieties and regrets lead to a fear of the appointment we can't reschedule: death. But like it or not, the statistics on death are still hovering around 100 percent. The fact is that we are all going to die. The Bible says that when we breathe our last breath on this planet and step into eternity, we will be launched into one of two places: either into heaven with the Lord, or into a Christless eternity in hell separated from God. What we do on this side, on earth, determines where we will spend eternity. It hinges on a decision that we all face right here, right now: either to accept and receive what God did for us through Christ or to reject it.

Perhaps you fear God. You know that God is supposed to be a loving God, but you still fear his judgment and wrath. You know the lifestyle you are currently engaged in does not square up with the pages of Scripture. You realize that your vocabulary, your thoughts, and the places you frequent do not really reflect the personal relationship you profess having with the Lord. Deep down you have this uneasy feeling that one day the accounts will be settled and your balance sheet will not come up to scratch. And you know that the kind of fear you have of God is not the same kind of godly fear the Bible says we should have. What does it mean, after all, to know the fear of God?

I don't mean to be a downer, but fear is real. I'm not telling you something that you don't already know, but fear is out there, and you are going to encounter it at some point in your life. And—here's the kicker—if you are making choices you know you shouldn't, then you have every good reason to have fears in your life. Let me repeat that: you may have good reason to be fearful. Often our own choices determine our level of fear. Bad choices most often bring discontentment, worries, and unrest. Good choices provide satisfaction, peace, and rest.

While many people fear what they do not understand or cannot control, those who have chosen to follow Christ have access to and belong to the one who does understand and is in control of everything. So many try, as Proverbs 3:5 warns against, to lean on their own understanding: "Trust in the LORD with all your heart and lean not on your own understanding." But this selfish and foolish choice leads to a path of cliffs, jags, and treacherous turns.

Proverbs 3:6 says, "In all your ways acknowledge him, and he will make your paths straight." By choosing to acknowledge the Lord—to observe his ways and know him personally—we can rest assured that he will walk the path ahead and make a better way for us.

This is not a psychological self-help book about how to cope with feelings of fear and anxiety. This book is about making right choices and then trusting God for the rest. It is about understanding the difference between relying on our own limited understanding and trusting in God's unlimited resources. When we trust God and do life his way, the biblical words of comfort, "Be of good cheer, I have overcome the world" (John 16:33 KJV) take on a new and profound meaning.

DAYS
OF TERROR

Fear of Helplessness

I was sitting in my office, preparing for our Tuesday morning staff meeting, when the phone call came in from my wife, Lisa. "Ed, turn your TV on," she said. I watched the news reports in a surreal daze as hijacked airliners knifed through the sky and crashed into the World Trade Towers and the Pentagon. Those planes hit major points of our culture—the major point of power and commerce in New York and the major point of protection and intelligence in Washington. The news was devastating and almost beyond belief. I will never forget exactly where I was the moment I heard the devastating news on Tuesday morning, September 11, 2001.

Since that time, I, along with millions of other Americans, have gone through a myriad of emotions. If you are like me, you have felt fear, anxiety, apprehension, and anger. I heard someone say, just shortly after the attacks, that it is almost like America has been on an extended emotional and nervous buzz. Around the gym where I work out, conversations are usually pretty jovial, with people talking

chapter 1

about how many reps they are doing, or a new diet they are trying, or sports, or the stock market. Over the days following the terrorist attacks, though, a holy hush enveloped the place. People were talking about soul issues, matters of life and death.

One man, who is not even a Christian, came up to me and said, "Ed, when I heard what happened, I just wanted to go home and hug my daughter." We naturally gravitate toward family and faith during times like these. It's amazing how those things in life which are truly most significant quickly bubble to the surface in the aftermath of tragedy.

We've been confronted over the past few months with a rising tide of national and individual fears in the unseen and unknown enemy of *terrorism*. Nonstop television coverage reminded us daily and hourly of the ever-present threat to our national security and personal liberty. As the smoke of the World Trade Center's toppled towers began to clear, deadly biological weapons showed up in envelopes mailed to news organizations and political leaders.

After receiving an anthrax-tainted letter in his office at CBS, Dan Rather tried to reassure a nervous television audience, "Our biggest problem is not anthrax . . . our biggest problem is fear."[1] Despite these and other words of reassurance about our safety, feelings of insecurity and helplessness seemed to take on a new shape with each passing day.

We've learned more in the last few months than we may ever care to know about the psychology of fear, in a myriad of newspaper and magazine articles on the subject. One *USA Today* writer summed it up this way: "Today in America, fear is a weapon. It is the knife that would sever our faith in each other, the club that would beat us into resignation, the gun that would stop us from fly-ing and buying."[2]

In another *USA Today* article, entitled "Our Nervous Nation," this fear of terrorism is characterized more generally as "fear of the unknown. We just don't know what is going to happen next."[3]

I think, though, that George Will has captured best the essence of what has happened to us as a nation since September 11: "Wielded with sufficient cunning, [terrorists] can spread the demor-alizing helplessness that is terrorism's most important intended by-product."[4] Most of all, we as Americans are terrified of losing control. Helplessness is just not in our vocabulary most of the time. And, when confronted with an enemy who uses deception and covert tactics to disrupt our normal, everyday, in-control lives, we feel a helplessness we have seldom felt before as the world's only remaining superpower. The control we thought we had is quickly exposed for what it really was: merely an illusion of control.

As I began to process some of these surreal events and resulting feelings, I did what I often do and wrote down some thoughts in my journal. Early one morning I took out my journal and, as I was watching the sunrise, I began to write down some things I believe God was teaching me through these times of national tragedy and uncertainty.

Journaling my prayers and recording my thoughts and feelings help me connect with God on a more personal level. As I thought about the feelings of helplessness and terror that were surfacing inside me and in the faces and words of others, I was reminded of several key principles from Scripture that help bring a renewed per-spective during these days of terror.

EVIL IS RAMPANT

The first thing I wrote down that morning was, "This tragedy reminds me that evil is rampant." What would cause a person or group of people to slaughter thousands of innocent people? What would cause someone, or a group of people, to wreak havoc and fear on an entire society with senseless acts of terror? A damaged chromosome? A poor family of origin? No, purely and simply, it is evil.

The people who perpetrated this act on September 11, 2001—and at other times in our recent past—are evil. Yes, we are all made in the image of God, but many people have so marred that image that they have become satanic. You don't have to be a great theologian to realize there is a personal, sinister, evil force out there wreaking havoc on this planet. You just have to open your eyes to the truth of what is happening all around us.

Following this tragic event, I was amazed at the wide range of explanations offered for the terrorists' actions, evidently to help us understand and accept how these evil people felt justified in what they did. Some commentators and scholars felt it was inappropriate for us to classify their actions as evil, claiming that evil is such a relative term. It is not helpful, they say, to call them evildoers, as the President did, but passionate zealots who, based on their own moral code, were carrying out their own sense of justice.

I have no doubt that terrorists justify their actions based on their own sense of right and wrong, just as all of mankind has done throughout history. But creating your own moral code to justify your actions does not negate the truth of God's Word and the absolute nature of morality. We need to recognize and call evil what it is, because that's the only way to view life from God's perspective.

The Bible is clear about the existence and nature of evil. The Bible says in Romans 3:23 that all of us have sinned and fall short of—or miss the mark of—the absolute standard of goodness, the glorious character of God. We have a downward gravitational pull— a bent toward badness that causes us to rebel against God and to go our own way. I have it in my life, and so do you. No one taught me how to lie, cheat, or steal. No one taught you how to do those bad things. You just know how to do them. When people come to a point, though, that they so turn their back on God, when they come to a point that they so mar the image of God, I truly believe they become satanic and capable of extreme acts of evil.

During times of crisis, people often ask me, "Ed, why? Why does God allow bad things like this to happen?" Any time you are dealing with a tragedy or time of crisis that you don't understand (and that includes most of them), this "why" question is a natural response. Well, I will tell you why, but you may not like the answer. Here it is: God allows evil in the world because he loves us.

Now, pay close attention, because I'm not saying that God loves evil or loves to inflict us with bad things. Quite the contrary: God has an absolutely perfect nature, and he loves to give us good things. One of the best things that God has given us from creation is a free will, the ability to choose both good and evil. Bad things happen and evil is rampant in the world because man has chosen to rebel against God from the very beginning. That rebellion is sin against a holy God.

The bad news is that because we are born with a sinful nature, we all have a natural propensity toward evil. The good news, though, is that God, through the death and resurrection of Jesus Christ, offers the forgiveness of sin to us. The greatest good that can ever happen in this world is for a man or a woman to choose, *of his or her own free will,* to trust Christ as Savior.

However, by giving us the free will to choose the greatest good, it means that the window for evil has to be opened as well. Man cannot truly be free without the ability to choose the opposite of what God has planned for him. God desires for us, as free creatures, to choose the greatest good, but he must also give us the opportunity to choose the opposite, the greatest of evil. Sadly, while given the chance to love, we have also been given the chance to hate.

We have an ultimate choice, to accept the love of God or to reject it. When we accept God's love, we are given the capacity to love him back. He does not force his love on us, nor does he force or coerce us to love him back. True love is not a forced love; we either choose to love God, or we don't. Those on our planet who choose to go the other way, who choose evil, can really get messed up. They can mar their image, and truly, I believe, take on the persona of the demonic. The Bible supports this in Romans 1:28–32:

> Furthermore, since they did not think it worthwhile to
> retain the knowledge of God, he gave them over to a
> depraved mind, to do what ought not to be done. They
> have become filled with every kind of wickedness, evil,
> greed and depravity. They are full of envy, murder, strife,
> deceit and malice. They are gossips, slanderers, God-
> haters, insolent, arrogant and boastful; they invent ways of

doing evil; they disobey their parents; they are senseless, faithless, heartless, ruthless. Although they know God's righteous decree that those who do such things deserve death, they not only continue to do these very things but also approve of those who practice them.

The path of the rebellious sinner is a sad one, and unfortunately we see evidence of many today that traverse this deadly road. Again, we are all sinners, but some have perverted God's law to such an extent that they have been "given over to a depraved mind, to do what ought not to be done." Some even do horrendous acts of evil and believe them, in their own depravity and warped sense of justice, to be acts of good. Such is the state of those who perpetrate acts of terror on civilian life in America today and around the world. They justify their own evil actions with the moral reasoning of a depraved mind.

EVIL DEMANDS AN APPROPRIATE RESPONSE

This may bring up another question in your mind, as you consider those who commit extreme acts of evil and terror, like the attack on September 11. I've addressed why evil happens in the world, but how should we respond to "evildoers," as President Bush has so often called terrorists?

Christ tells us that we are to pray for our enemies and to love our enemies: "But I tell you who hear me: Love your enemies, do good to those who hate you, bless those who curse you, pray for those who mistreat you" (Luke 6:27–28). Our individual response and response as a church should be to pray for people who rebel against

God and seek to destroy us, even to such a degree as to cause the kind of horror we have seen in recent days.

There is also, however, an appropriate response from the government which defends our lives and freedoms. Make no mistake, the Bible also tells us that sin has a consequence, both eternally and in the present. Romans 6:23 says, "For the wages of sin is death." Those who continue down the path of sin and death face both the limited judgment of earthly authority and the infinite judgment of God in eternity.

God has placed the government in authority over us, and the government has a biblical mandate to seek justice of those who would terrorize and seek to destroy the freedoms we enjoy under God. When our freedom has become threatened, we have to stand up and fight.

Romans 13:1–2, 4–5 speaks of this biblical mandate: "Everyone must submit himself to the governing authorities, for there is no authority except that which God has established. The authorities that exist have been established by God" (v. 1). We must understand that God has established a chain of command in everything. There is a chain of command in the home, at school, in churches, in office complexes and companies, in God's kingdom. God has established the authorities that exist, the Bible says. "Consequently, he who rebels against the authority is rebelling against what God has instituted, and those who do so will bring judgment on themselves" (v. 2).

Continuing in verse 4, the "he" refers to God's authority over us, be it king, prince, president, or prime minister: "For he is God's servant to do you good. But if you do wrong, be afraid, for he does not bear the sword for nothing. He is God's servant"—we are talking about the government now—"an agent of wrath to bring punishment on the wrongdoer." This is, I believe, a New Testament defense for the use of force against terrorists and other enemies of freedom.

Paul concludes in verse 5: "Therefore, it is necessary to submit to the authorities, not only because of possible punishment but also because of conscience." It is evident that many people in this world have lost their consciences, their ability to reason morally. When their conscience does not bring them into submission, it is the government's right and responsibility to use the sword of judgment to bring them into submission. Yes, I continue to pray for our enemies, as should all Christians. But we must not forget our responsibility as a nation to defend freedom by bringing swift and exact judgment when appropriate.

Evil is rampant. We see microcosms of mayhem throughout our culture—rape, murder, envy, pride, jealousy—and the ugly list goes on. And, on Tuesday morning, September 11, 2001, we saw evil on a grand and horrible scale. We are all sinners. Those of us who know Christ are saved by grace through faith. Those who have not come into a relationship with him have turned their backs on God, some to such an extent that they have been given over to the devil.

The bottom line, however, is that we should take comfort in the fact that God does not bring evil on us. All evil and tragedy can be traced to the effects of a fallen world inhabited by fallen creatures that have chosen to rebel against a holy and loving God.

GOD IS IN CONTROL

I also reflected in my journal that morning that "God is in control." Evil is rampant, as wanton acts of terror so poignantly remind us, but God has not lost control of the universe. Theologians call this the sovereignty of God. In other words, God was not shocked or taken by surprise at what occurred on Tuesday morning, September 11. Quite frankly, the fact that these extreme acts of evil do not happen with more regularity is evidence of the power and protection of God in the world today.

It is a supernatural restraining of the Holy Spirit of God that crazier things don't happen more often. One day, I believe, we will see a world in upheaval and all of the forces of hell unleashed. This will happen before the Lord comes back to establish his reign. But the terror we experience today is just a brief little comparison, a microcosm, of what is going to happen on a grander scale in the future. Even then, though, God will ultimately control the fate of the world and bring all things to a climactic conclusion under the reign of Christ. The psalmist declared in Psalm 103:19, "The LORD has established his throne in heaven, and his kingdom rules over all." God is calling the shots; he knows the future. We don't have to worry.

I grew up in Columbia, South Carolina. Because we lived on a dirt road, I always considered it "the country." Across the dirt road from our place was a stretch of woods, and in the middle of the woods was a little lake. One evening, we wanted to watch the South Carolina sunset over the lake. I remember that I was in the fifth grade at the time. That evening Dad and I walked down the little path carved through the woods, and we stood on the bank of this lake and watched the sunset.

Out of the blue, Dad asked, "Son, do you want to see a big water moccasin?"

I said, "Yes, sir, I do."

He pointed toward the bank, "Look, Ed." Sure enough, right on the bank was a five-foot water moccasin—big, thick, and muscular. This snake was so thick he had a goatee, I think.

I said, "Wow, that's a big snake, Dad." I looked to my right and asked, "Dad, is that another one?"

Dad looked and said, "Son, I think it is. That's really interesting. We have seen two big snakes in thirty seconds. Wow."

Then I said, "Dad, is that another one?"

I don't know what happened. I'm not sure if the water moccasins were in some kind of mating frenzy, but we saw fifty water moccasins within a matter of minutes. They were on the bank, around our feet, in the water. I was terrified. I was beginning to panic and wondered if we would get out of there alive.

I'll never forget what my father said: "Son, jump on my back. Jump on my back."

I didn't have to take a running start. My vertical leap at that moment would have embarrassed Vince Carter or Kobe Bryant. I jumped on his back and will never forget grabbing him and burying my face in his shirt. I clung to his strong back as he shone his tiny flashlight on the winding path and negotiated our safe exit around all those snakes.

It was like an Indiana Jones movie, but I wasn't going to stay and wait for the credits to roll. I remember being so relieved as my dad found the path and took us home. At that moment, my dad could have walked on water as far as I was concerned. I'll never, ever forget that experience. I knew Daddy was in control of the situation.

Many of us in America today are living in fear. As turmoil, apprehension, and anxiety begin to make us feel trapped, as if there's no way out, our heavenly Father says, "Come on. Jump on my back. I am in control. Jump on my back. I will shine my light on your situation and take you through. I will walk with you and show you where the path is. I will take you home."

Are you on your way home? Are you riding on your heavenly Father's back? When life seems out of control and feelings of helplessness surround you on every side, God is still in control and can carry you safely through. That does not mean you won't experience hardships or tragedies, that you will somehow be immune to the effects of evil in the world. But it does mean that, no matter what happens, you know and are holding on to the one who holds the future in his hands.

Don't go it alone by saying, "No, God, I'll just do my own thing. I can handle this situation, God. I can do it. I can make it without your help. I can muster up enough courage to do it." No, you can't. In one of the most beloved passages of Scripture, the psalmist reminds us that the only sure guide on the path of life is the Good Shepherd:

The LORD is my shepherd, I shall not be in want.

He makes me lie down in green pastures,

he leads me beside quiet waters,

he restores my soul.

He guides me in paths of righteousness

for his name's sake. (Ps. 23:1–3)

The path may be uncertain, but the way home is clear in the arms of our heavenly Father. God will lead us down the right path, the path of righteousness, if we will follow him completely and without reservation.

LIFE IS FRAGILE

I was reminded of something else as I contemplated the events of September 11, and I recorded this in my journal: "This tragedy reminds me that life is fragile." Wouldn't you agree? Those thousands of people who got up Tuesday morning, sipped their coffee, read the paper, dropped their children off, entered those World Trade Towers, stepped into the Pentagon, and boarded those hijacked airplanes. Little did they realize that they were stepping from this life to the next. They didn't realize that it was their last day on this planet. They had no clue what that fateful day held for them.

We are the only species that can actually anticipate our death. We know we have an appointment one day that we can't put off. We do not know when; only God does. But it is going to happen. My houseplants don't anticipate their deaths. My four dogs, which weigh a combined total of 440 pounds, don't anticipate their deaths. As human beings, though, with a sense of consciousness and an awareness of our own existence, we know all too well that some day we are going to die.

One of the great ironies of life is that we are not really prepared to live until we are prepared to die. Are you prepared to die? If you died right now, do you know where you would go? Is your eternal destination secure? Are you riding on the back of your heavenly Father, or are you trying to do life solo?

James 4:13–14 talks about the frailty of life: "Now listen, you who say, 'Today or tomorrow we will go to this or that city, spend a

21

year there, carry on business and make money.' Why, you do not even know what will happen tomorrow. What is your life? You are a mist that appears for a little while and then vanishes." You are one germ away, one drunk driver away, or one blood clot away from eternity. We will spend more time on the other side of the grave than on this side of the grave. Yet the choices we make on this side of the grave determine our eternal destination.

We are creatures who have a free will, and we all have a choice to make. Tragedy has a way of bringing us back to reality. September 11 was a wake-up call for those of us who call ourselves believers. It's a wake-up call for us to get serious about understanding the implications of walking with the Lord. It's a wake-up call for us to capture those kingdom moments, when so many people around us who don't know Christ are asking those deep questions—questions of the soul.

It is also a wake-up call for those who are not Christians. If you have been testing the waters of faith, it's time to make a decision. Eternity may be closer than you think. You may have been drawn to church in recent months because you have this hole in your heart that you can't explain. You may have seen the title of this book and picked it up for the same reason. You can't seem to get rid of the nagging fears in your life, and you are searching desperately for peace and contentment.

You may have questions and doubts about your eternal destiny. And, despite your efforts to make sense of it all, you have not been able to find the meaning of life. Tragic events have a way of knocking us down on one knee, emotionally or relationally or in some other realm. I think God would say, "Put the other knee down and give me your life and your worship." Put the other knee down and say, "God, have your way in my life."

The weekend after the attacks in New York and Washington, record numbers of people flooded into churches across our land. Do you know why? Churches were bulging at the seams because the other "houses of worship" were closed down. The football stadiums and baseball stadiums that are usually packed every weekend with adoring fans were closed. And people suddenly lost interest in taking their usual weekend excursions to their lake homes or on their cabin cruisers. The gods of sports and leisure fell miserably short of bringing real satisfaction.

God says to have no other gods before him, yet we are worshiping other gods. We spend more money on pornography and cosmetics than we do on the things of God, and we wonder what is wrong with America? When the most dangerous place for a baby to be today is in its mother's womb, something is dreadfully wrong with our priorities. Where have we gone wrong? We need to repent of breaking the first commandment. We need to say, "God, I am a miserable sinner and have not been putting you first in my life. I need to change my life. God, I want to do a 180-degree turn, and only the power of Christ can make it happen."

The twin towers in New York represented everything America stands for—wealth and commerce and power. Yet they crumbled in a few short minutes. On one particular news report, rescue workers reported that the first fifteen stories of that massive structure crumbled down to just one foot of dust and ash.[5] This is hard to fathom, but true: fifteen stories, representing hundreds of tons of steel and concrete, reduced to just one foot of rubble.

The Bible says that one day we will stand before God, and everything in our lives that has not been built on Jesus Christ and his church will crumble. Think about the billions and billions of dollars of business deals that were being transacted and planned that day when those towers crumbled. Think about the incredible technology in those buildings—technology that many hail as the savior of modern culture. The business deals ground to a halt, and the technology failed, and within an hour or so America was knocked to a knee. It's time for America to put the other knee down.

Now, please understand me here: I'm not saying that God caused the attack on New York and Washington, as some sort of judgment so America would repent. It is God's prerogative to judge when and where he will, and I do not presume to know his sovereign will in these matters. But I do know from his Word that God uses catalyzing events like this to bring people to him, to remind them of important realities in life. Jesus talked about one of these realities in Matthew 7:24–27:

> Therefore everyone who hears these words of mine and
> puts them into practice is like a wise man who built his house
> on the rock. The rain came down, the streams rose, and the
> winds blew and beat against that house; yet it did not fall,
> because it had its foundation on the rock. But everyone who
> hears these words of mine and does not put them into prac-
> tice is like a foolish man who built his house on sand. The
> rain came down, the streams rose, and the winds blew and
> beat against that house, and it fell with a great crash.

Christ was talking about an eternal foundation here. He was finishing the Sermon on the Mount, and he was contrasting those who are authentic disciples of his with those who are not. Those who do obey his teaching are like the wise man who builds on rock, and those who do not obey him are like the follish man who builds on sand

Prior to this section in Matthew, Jesus had just finished a sobering indictment on those who profess to be believers but are not true followers of him. They call on the name of the Lord, and they have all the right moves, at least from a distance, but deep down they are standing on a sandy foundation.

When the next storm hits, when the ensuing tragedy strikes, they will crumble. They are nothing more than "storefront followers," with just some flashy samples of the merchandise so they can look good to others. But if you go into the store to buy some produce, there is nothing there. Jesus says that the lives of such people produce no fruit. Only by the fruit they produce can we know who his true disciples are.

Many people today are building their lives on treacherous foundations. Their lives are characterized by inner fears because they are one storm away from disaster. They have the trappings of religion, but there is no genuine fruit to indicate any evidence of an authentic relationship with Jesus Christ. Their lives are built instead on power or wealth or status or family and country. Yes, family and country can become idols if they become the foundations of our lives. Much evil has been done in the name of familial or national honor, including the recent acts of terror.

Nothing should replace our allegiance to Jesus Christ. Family and nation remain strong only when individuals within them have built their lives on a firm foundation, the rock of Jesus Christ. No other allegiance is as lasting as this one, and none other should take its place in our hearts.

Many Americans today face the same choices that Solomon of old faced. Solomon, the grandest of Israel's kings, took a free fall into a forty-year abyss of partying. This sovereign was wealthier than we could ever imagine, and he used his great wealth and power to try everything "under the sun." He had seven hundred concubines at his beck and call. He sampled the finest wines and the best of foods. He built expansive buildings inlayed with the purest gold and the rarest of jewels. You name it; he did it.

Near the end of his life, this is what Solomon said, because he tried to do all of these things by himself, away from God: "Yet when I surveyed all that my hands had done and what I had toiled to achieve, everything was meaningless, a chasing after the wind; nothing was gained under the sun" (Eccles. 2:11).

First Timothy 6:7 reiterates the sentiment, "For we brought nothing into the world, and we can take nothing out of it." All of our achievements and acquisitions become meaningless when weighed on the scales of eternity. And often it takes an event of awful proportions to bring us to our senses. Through a crisis of fear, we turn to the things that really matter in life. In the blink of an eye, many people realize how fragile life is and wake up to a spiritual reality they have worked hard to ignore.

Even the irreligious, during times of crisis, suddenly turn to faith and family. I saw on the news that Madonna, before one of her concerts following the September 11 tragedy, led in a prayer. And MTV, a network that has been blaspheming the name of God for years, asked America to pray for the victims and their families.

News anchors, from Dan Rather to Tom Brockaw, have asked us to pray. Before September 11, 2001, you could be prosecuted for praying in schools, but afterwards, on the front page of newspapers across the country, we read that students and teachers alike were praying in schools.

Don't get me wrong. Prayer is desperately needed in this country, and I'm glad that we are turning to God during these times of uncertainty. But we should not wait for a crisis before we face the facts of our mortal existence and finally decide to get things right with our maker. We must be honest with ourselves and face the truth of our mortality.

Ernest Becker, in his Pulitzer Prize-winning book *The Denial of Death,* said it this way: "We arrange our lives, we human beings, around ignoring or avoiding or oppressing the most irrefutable fact in the whole world, which is, 'I'm going to die.' You're going to die."[6] Don't ignore death or the fragility of your existence. Prepare to die by placing your eternity in the hands of God, so you can begin at long last to really live.

God Is Trustworthy

Why can we trust our eternal destiny to God? Quite simply, because God is trustworthy. Do you know what the word *trust* means? Our English word *trust* comes from an Indo-European root word meaning "to be solid," which is also the source of our word *tree.* If you want to be firmly planted, if you want to have deep roots, if you want to do life like a tree, then trust. And only God is worthy of our trust.

One section of Scripture, which I mentioned in the introduction, has been the theme Scripture for the Young family for generations. It's Proverbs 3:5–6: "Trust in the LORD with all your heart and lean not on your own understanding; in all your ways acknowledge him, and he will make your paths straight."

When we lean on our own understanding, we are in trouble. We are powerless. When we lean on God's understanding—lean into his love—we are powerful. What a message of hope. How do we trust God? One of the most powerful ways is to pray. When we pray, we are admitting our shortcomings and submitting to his will.

I am thrilled about America coming together and praying. I am happy that MTV is talking about prayer and that Tom Brockaw and Dan Rather are talking about prayer. More than ever before, people everywhere are praying for peace in our time. My hope, though, is that we will all pray to the one true God for peace *with* God, through the power and intercession of his Son, Jesus Christ. And that we will continue in prayer even after the crisis has passed.

Philippians 4:6–7 says: "Do not be anxious about anything, but in everything . . ." Does this say just in tragedies? Does this say just in catastrophic things? Does this say just when you are getting ready to close the big deal or undergo major surgery? No, it says, "In everything, by prayer and petition, with thanksgiving, present your requests to God." And then look at what will happen: "And the *peace of God,* which transcends all understanding, will guard your hearts and minds in Christ Jesus" (v. 7, emphasis added).

Everyone wants peace, don't they? We hear cries for civil, interracial, national, and international peace almost every day. But the peace that Paul speaks of here is an inner peace for those who belong to Christ, for those who have been reconciled to God through his Son. If God's peace is going to "guard your hearts and your minds in Christ Jesus," then you must first of all be *in*

Christ. If you want to have the peace of God, you must have peace *with* God.

We were born at war with God, and this war that is raging in the spiritual realm sets our desires against God's. We want to go our own way. We want to do what makes us feel good, what gives us pleasure, and what makes us look good. That's our sin nature, to desire that which is contrary to what God wants for us. But through his grace and mercy, God has taken the initiative to end the war. He has made a way to bring our desires into harmony with his desires.

God offers us a cease-fire in this spiritual struggle. Because of his love for us as self-centered sinners, he sent Christ as a sin sacrifice on our behalf. Through the death and resurrection of Jesus Christ, he has given us the opportunity to be reconciled to him and to resolve the conflict.

One day years ago because I had gone my own way, I was knocked down to one knee. I realized the folly of trying to do life without God. I put the other knee down and said, "God, I am going your way. I am going to trust Christ. I am going to accept Jesus into my life." That is why I have the peace of God, because I have peace *with* God. You may be able to say, "I, too, have the peace of God, because I have made peace *with* God by receiving the amazing grace of Jesus."

If you have done that, good for you. That is the greatest thing you could have ever done. If you haven't, why don't you trust Christ right now?

Would it shock you to know that, in an interview conducted on the street, when asked, "How does a person get to heaven?" most people responded, "I don't know." A video survey like this was conducted a couple of years ago by Fellowship Church. The vast majority of respondents said they did not know how to get to heaven. In fact, not one person was able to articulate what God says in the Bible about this important question.

Do you know the answer to this question? Are you like many of the people interviewed in this survey? Although they said they really didn't know the answer, many of them made guesses about how to get to heaven, based on what they had heard from others or perhaps on what they had always assumed. Some of the answers are as follows:

- "You just have to do your best."
- "If you are a good person and treat people well."
- "I guess you have to pray."
- "Just be nice, like good karma, to everyone."
- "You have to think of others instead of yourselves."

Do any of these responses sound familiar to you? You've probably heard other people say things like these, or perhaps you've even thought them yourself. But God has a different answer to this question. His answer is found in the Bible, God's Word to us.

God loves you. First of all, you need to understand that God loves you and wants to have a relationship with you. In fact, that is what heaven is all about; it is spending an eternity with God, in his presence. God says in 1 John 4:10, "This is love: not that we loved God, but that he loved us." He loves you so much that he created you with a free will, an ability to make choices. He knew that love could not be forced so he made it possible for mankind to accept or reject him.

Sin separates us from God. From the very beginning, though, man, out of pride, rejected God or rebelled against him. This rebellion is called sin. Because sin entered the world through that initial rebellion against God, all of us are sinners; we are born sinners. Romans 3:23 says, "For all have sinned and fall short of the glory of God." This is the problem that must be overcome in order to go to heaven. God is holy; he is perfect in every way. Because God is perfect, he cannot tolerate sin.

Sin demands a payment. Romans 6:23 tells us that sin demands a payment: "For the wages of sin is death." God does not condemn us for our sin. We are condemned already because we are sinners. Our sin keeps us from a relationship with God and demands a payment. That payment is death—physical death and spiritual separation from God for eternity.

Let's review the problem again: God loves us, but sin, our rebellion against a perfect God, keeps us from having that relationship now and forever in a place called heaven. Now that you understand the problem, let's talk about the solution. Because we are powerless in our own efforts to reach God (remember we are born sinners and cannot live a perfect life), God has reached down to us and made a way for us to be forgiven of our sins so we can have a relationship with God.

God has made the payment for us. Because sin demands a payment and we are not able to make that payment ourselves, God had to make the payment for us. He did this by sending his one and only Son, Jesus Christ, to die in our place on a cross so we could be forgiven of our sin against God. Jesus took our place; he was our substitute. Another way to look at this is that Jesus bridged the gap between God and us.

Think about the Golden Gate Bridge in California. This great bridge spans a body of water that stands between two land masses.

It is quite possible that people lost their lives in the construction of that bridge. But because of their sacrifice, people and all sorts of vehicles can pass unhindered from one side to the other. The chasm, the gap, was bridged.

Christ has done that for us: he has bridged the gap. The last part of 1 John 4:10 talks about this sacrifice on our behalf: "This is love: not that we loved God, but that he loved us *and sent his Son as an atoning sacrifice for our sins*" (emphasis added). God looked at what Christ did for us and accepted his death as an appropriate sacrifice for the sins of the world.

Christ's death satisfied the demands of sin; it paid the price in full. Romans 5:8 also explains this: "But God demonstrates his own love for us in this: While we were still sinners, Christ died for us." And three days after Christ died, he rose from the dead to break the power of death and the grave.

You can be saved by faith. Because Christ died for us, in our place, we can be "saved" from the penalty of sin. Remember, the penalty of sin is death, both physical and spiritual. Christ's death saves us from an eternity in hell without God. The Bible tells us that our bodies will some day be resurrected and made new. Christ's death paid the penalty for sin; Christ's resurrection from the dead broke the power of death, so we could live forever with God in heaven.

Christ has given us a great gift by dying in our place and then rising from the dead. And this gift demands a response from us. Once again, because God has created us with a free will, we have a choice to accept or reject Christ's gift—his payment for sin on our behalf.

The Bible says that the appropriate response is faith, simple faith: "For it is by grace you have been saved, through faith—and this is not from yourselves, it is the gift of God—not by works, so that no one can boast" (Eph. 2:8–9). God has extended his grace to us by sending Christ to die for us. Grace means that he has offered something to us that we don't deserve; it is God's unmerited favor toward us.

God is waiting for a response from you and from all humanity. He has extended his hand toward us by offering a way for us to be forgiven of sin and to have an eternal relationship with him. We don't deserve it, but God loves us so much that he has offered this as a way to bridge the insurmountable chasm between God and us.

What is your response? God has made the gift available, but you must take it by faith. Let's say that someone bought you a gift at Christmas and put it under the tree for you. But because you were too proud to accept the gift, you left it under the tree unopened. Did you accept that gift? Were you able to use that gift and make it yours? No. The gift must be received and opened before it becomes yours.

The real issue here is one of faith. Is there anything right now that is keeping you from believing that Christ died for you, that he is the Son of God, and that he has satisfied God's demand for a payment for sins? If you believe this, then you have become a child of God. Through Christ, you have been made perfect in God's eyes, because your sins have been, as the Bible calls it, "washed away." When God looks at you now, he sees Christ's perfection.

If you have accepted God's gift of forgiveness, through faith in Christ's death and resurrection, why don't you tell God right now about that. These words don't save you from sin, but they provide a way for you to talk to God and to profess the faith that is already in your heart. God knows what's in your heart, but he likes it when we talk to him.

If you've trusted in Jesus Christ, pray something like this to God: "Jesus Christ, I admit to you the obvious, that I have gone my own way. I have rebelled against you. I have leaned on my own understanding. I want to do an about-face. I want to repent and turn to you. I want to lean on your love, and I am placing the other knee down in humility before you. I am placing my trust in Christ, who died for me and then rose again, to save me from my sins and give me eternal life in heaven."

In these uncertain times that are filled with fearful and unsettling circumstances, God has promised to bring peace. The peace he brings can be found in the life of every person who is in Christ. Placing your faith in Christ is the first step in confronting the fears that beset us on every side. Even in these days of terror, when the very foundations of our society seem to be under attack, we can know the peace that surpasses all understanding by being reconciled to God through Christ.

The secular mind, deceived by every kind of humanistic philosophy, does not understand this kind of peace. The leaders of this world strive for political peace, while the spiritual peace that Christ offers eludes them. Even the leaders of the major world religions don't understand it, because they do not accept the one from which all real peace flows. They have not made him their own and thus do not understand the peace that only God can give through him.

Did you hear the first reaction of many of the people in New York and Washington when they saw those planes hitting the buildings?

They all said, "Oh, my God!" This has become such a natural and common phrase that it has all but lost its meaning. Why is this? It is because people are using it in vain, meaning they are calling upon and claiming a God that is not really theirs to claim. They live in rebellion toward him, day in and day out, and then call on his name only when a crisis hits or a tragedy happens.

If you want to be able to call on God when the tough times come, you need to allow him to possess you all the time. You must give your life into his control and allow him to infuse your life with the peace that will carry you through even the worst of times.

Is God *your* God? Has he possessed you? Do you know the peace of God? Have you chosen him and allowed him to possess you? Can you say, "Oh, my God?" and mean it. We have "In God we trust" on our American money. Do you really trust God, or is it just kind of a cliché, like "God bless America" or "God bless you."

We need to continue to pray for our leaders, for our nation, and for the peace process around the world. But the only way we can truly begin to confront our fears is by individually turning in repentance toward God and admitting, "God, I have had other gods before you. You are God. I am not. I am going to revolve my life from this day forward around those things that bring glory to you." Then and only then will we find the peace we seek—peace that will help us face our fears in these days of terror.

Take the first step in confronting your fears. Jump on God's back, trust him with your life, and allow him to navigate the uncertain and winding path of life. And he will take you home.

Facing Life's Phobias

EVIL IS RAMPANT

- Furthermore, since they did not think it worthwhile to retain the knowledge of God, he gave them over to a depraved mind, to do what ought not to be done. They have become filled with every kind of wickedness, evil, greed and depravity. They are full of envy, murder, strife, deceit and malice. They are gossips, slanderers, God-haters, insolent, arrogant and boastful; they invent ways of doing evil; they disobey their parents; they are senseless, faithless, heartless, ruthless. Although they know God's righteous decree that those who do such things deserve death, they not only continue to do these very things but also approve of those who practice them (Rom. 1:28–32).

EVIL DEMANDS AN APPROPRIATE RESPONSE

- "But I tell you who hear me: Love your enemies, do good to those who hate you, bless those who curse you, pray for those who mistreat you" (Luke 6:27–28).
- Everyone must submit himself to the governing authorities, for there is no authority except that which God has established. The authorities that exist have been established by God. Consequently, he who rebels against the authority is rebelling against what God has instituted, and those who do so will bring judgment on themselves. . . . For he is God's servant to do you good. But if you do wrong, be afraid, for he does not bear the sword for nothing. He is God's servant,

an agent of wrath to bring punishment on the wrongdoer. Therefore, it is necessary to submit to the authorities, not only because of possible punishment but also because of conscience (Rom. 13:1–2; 4–5).

GOD IS IN CONTROL

- The LORD has established his throne in heaven, and his kingdom rules over all (Ps. 103:19).
- The LORD is my shepherd, I shall not be in want.
  He makes me lie down in green pastures,
    he leads me beside quiet waters,
    he restores my soul.
  He guides me in paths of righteousness
    for his name's sake (Ps. 23:1–3).

LIFE IS FRAGILE

- Now listen, you who say, "Today or tomorrow we will go to this or that city, spend a year there, carry on business and make money." Why, you do not even know what will happen tomorrow. What is your life? You are a mist that appears for a little while and then vanishes (James 4:13–14).
- "Therefore everyone who hears these words of mine and puts them into practice is like a wise man who built his house on the rock. The rain came down, the streams rose, and the winds blew and beat against that house; yet it did not fall, because it had its foundation on the rock. But everyone who hears these words of mine and does not put them into practice is like a foolish man who built his house on sand. The rain came

down, the streams rose, and the winds blew and beat against that house, and it fell with a great crash" (Matt. 7:24–27).

- For we brought nothing into the world, and we can take nothing out of it (1 Tim. 6:7).

GOD IS TRUSTWORTHY

- Trust in the LORD with all your heart and lean not on your own understanding; in all your ways acknowledge him, and he will make your paths straight (Prov. 3:5–6).

- Do not be anxious about anything, but in everything, by prayer and petition, with thanksgiving, present your requests to God. And the peace of God, which transcends all understanding, will guard your hearts and minds in Christ Jesus (Phil. 4:6–7).

- *Sin separates us from God.* For all have sinned and fall short of the glory of God (Rom. 3:23).

- *Sin demands a payment.* For the wages of sin is death (Rom. 6:23).

- *God has made the payment for us.* This is love: not that we loved God, but that he loved us and sent his Son as an atoning sacrifice for our sins (1 John 4:10). But God demonstrates his own love for us in this: While we were still sinners, Christ died for us (Rom. 5:8).

- *You can be saved by faith.* For it is by grace you have been saved, through faith—and this is not from yourselves, it is the gift of God—not by works, so that no one can boast (Eph. 2:8–9).

FUTURE FRIGHT

Fear of the Future

Everything these days is going retro: shoes, clothes, food, and cars. I looked in my daughter's closet the other day and almost fainted when I realized that half of her clothes were the same kinds of things my wife wore when we were dating. We are good at borrowing stuff from the past and regurgitating it in the present. If you feel like your clothes are out of style, don't throw them away. Just wait a few years, pull those old clothes back out, and you will probably be right back in the swing of things.

We recycle and replay other things from our past as well. These things are not very positive, and they have the ability to keep us down and even cripple us in the future. The past is a tricky aspect of our lives that requires careful handling, because it can either feed our hopes and dreams for the future or starve them.

If you have heard me speak or read any of my books, you know that I talk a lot about my dogs. I have two huge bull mastiffs named Brute and Apollo. I feed them, as you would imagine, every day. Brute is the younger dog; he weighs about 150 pounds. I put Brute's

chapter 2

food out first. Then I have to give Apollo, the older one, his food around the corner.

Apollo, though the smaller of the two—weighing in at about 145 pounds—is clearly the dominant dog. When he has finished gulping down his food, he will run over to Brute's dish, knock Brute away, and start eating from there too.

Brute is big enough and strong enough to stand his ground, but the memory of being dominated when he was a pup holds him back. Because Brute is younger, regardless of his current weight advantage, he still feels inferior to Apollo. Engrained in his behavior and habits is the belief that he is still smaller and therefore less powerful. It is the fear of Apollo from long ago, when Apollo was bigger and more powerful, that keeps him from being nourished in the present.

Going retro like Brute keeps us focused on the wrong things. If we remember the bad stuff from the past—the evil stuff, the mistakes—it can freeze us in the present and hurt our prospects for the future. We look back and say to ourselves, "I will never forget that comment someone made about my personality or my looks. I really regret what I did in that relationship, and I'm not sure I can move on. I remember how I have messed up so many times. Surely, God can't use me. He can't possibly make something positive out of all this and feed me in the present." It's a fear of the future being fed by fears from the past.

These inner emotions and memories that tend to starve our potential often come from hurtful words and circumstances of childhood. Every negative memory from those early days is seared into our minds as if with a hot branding iron. Not feeling accepted, never feeling good enough at sports or school, harsh words from peers, or—for those from broken homes—the belief that they somehow caused the breakup of their parents. These negative emotions from long ago creep into our consciousness over and over again until we begin to succumb to their draining influence in our lives.

The past is not all bad, however. Both the positive and negative experiences from the past can be used by God to build us up, to prepare us for a stronger future. Going retro—if we focus on the lessons we have learned and the provision of God through both good times and bad—can be good; it can make us strong. Remembering what God has done, how he has helped us, assisted us, and picked us up when we felt low, is a positive and life-sustaining thing. Positive emotions and memories, as well as an understanding of how God has used negative emotions and memories to help us grow, can cause us to stand firm and be nourished in the present.

STAND FIRM

Remember the children of Israel? They often found it difficult to use the past in a positive way. Either they would distort the negative aspects of their bondage and thereby discount their miraculous deliverance at God's hand, or they would forget all the good things God had done for them.

God miraculously delivered them from hundreds of years of slavery in Egypt. Through the ten plagues that eventually led to their freedom, he proved his power and glory time after time. After all that God had done for them, you would think they would go retro and remember all of the supernatural acts of God from the past when they found themselves pressed up against the Red Sea by the pursuing Egyptian army. You would expect them to trust God to deliver them once again from the hands of their enemies.

But the Israelites went retro in a negative light and began to whine and moan. Instead of looking back and praising God for what he had done for them, they blamed God and Moses for putting them in another life-threatening predicament, for taking them away from their comfort zone of slavery and into the wilderness of new opportunities.

They actually looked back on their slavery and oppression as a better time. They were trapped by their past memories and their narrow perspectives. They wanted the security of their dysfunctional safety net. They did not trust God to be able to take those negative experiences and make something better out of their lives.

In short, they were fearful of what lay ahead because it was out of their control and out of their normal parameters of thought. Their physical oppression had led to oppressive thinking, and this mentality was all they knew. They were unwilling to move beyond the engrained emotions and memories that defined them.

This distorted view of the past led to negativity toward the promise of the future. These negative emotions, based on an unrealistic and unhealthy past perspective, produced a future fear that demonstrated itself in whining, complaining, and moaning: "Oh, Moses, why did you bring us here? We were better off in slavery, Moses, better off the way we used to be. We never should have followed you!"

It is easy for us to look at their circumstances and say, "That's unbelievable! How could these hardheaded people complain to the Almighty God? They need a major reality check." But we shouldn't be too critical of these stubborn Israelites.

In the midst of these negative emotions, Moses stepped in and said, "Do not be afraid. Stand firm and you will see the deliverance the LORD will bring you today. The Egyptians you see today you will never see again. The LORD will fight for you; you need only to be still" (Exod. 14:13–14).

Wouldn't you like to have a Moses in your life to tell you something like that every time those negative emotions creep up—when you feel trapped by your past or you fear the uncertainty of the future? What an encouragement those words must have been to the people of Israel on that infamous day in history.

The beauty of Moses' words is that they are just as appropriate and beneficial to us today as they were back then. God's message of hope has not changed: "Stand firm and see the deliverance of the Lord."

When you feel fear overshadow you, stand firm. The Bible says, "Be still, and know that I am God" (Ps. 46:10). We can be reminded through his Word and through those gentle reminders from the Holy Spirit of what God has done for us. God will bring to our minds those experiences in the past where he cared for us and delivered us. This will give us the drive and the motivation to be nourished in the present.

Do you feel like an Egyptian army is pursuing you? Do you feel pressed up against a Red Sea? Are you whining and moaning, "I would be better off if things were the way they used to be. I've messed up too much for God to deliver me this time. I'm afraid of what might happen in the future." Be still and listen to the voice of God. Go retro and remember the salvation of the Lord, and then take those good memories of God's deliverance and faithfulness into the future.

TAKE THE NEXT STEP

Being still, or standing firm, doesn't mean we do nothing while we wait on God. Faith requires action. As we trust God with the future, we need to be taking the next step along the path. Too many times we are overwhelmed with the future because we try to see too far ahead. All that God requires of us is to take the next step. We know that ultimately he holds the future in his hands. But he reveals only what we need to know, where we need to go, one footfall of faith at a time.

Look again at Exodus 14:15. God replied to Moses and responded to the Israelites' whining, "Why are you crying out to me?" God is a very patient God, and he is slow to anger, and his mercy never ceases. But even God sometimes looks down at all of our whining and complaining and declares, "What is up with you? Have I not proven myself enough to you at this point? I am tired of your crying."

Yes, God grows weary of our lack of faith and of the pity parties we throw ourselves. Instead of our cries, he wants some action. He wants us to take the next step, trusting that he will continue to lead us down the path of deliverance.

God continued speaking to Moses: "Tell the Israelites to move on. Raise your staff and stretch out your hand over the sea to divide the water so that the Israelites can go through the sea on dry ground" (Exod. 14:15–16). Before God even told Moses to raise his staff and divide the sea, he told the Israelites to "move on." God told them to move it, when Moses had just told them to be still and stand firm. What are we to make of this seeming contradiction in orders?

This was not a contradiction in commands. Moses was address-ing the people's inner turmoil when he told them to be still. They were terrified, and they thought they had been brought into the desert to die. The stranglehold of fear had trapped their inner resolve, and Moses was telling them to be at peace, knowing that God would not let them down. He was telling them to still the con-flicting thoughts in their minds, to let the peace of God permeate their hearts, and to know that God was still God. Nothing had changed as far as God was concerned; he had brought his people this far and was not about to let them die.

This was also a word from Moses in reaction to their desire to go backward instead of moving forward. The fight-or-flight mechanism was telling them to flee, to run back into the arms of their oppres-sors and to beg for mercy. God had another plan. He was going to fight for them and take them forward to a land he had promised them, a land of freedom and opportunity for his people. Moses was encouraging them to squelch their natural instincts and to stand firm against the basic reaction to take flight, to run away from the obstacles before them.

God's response, on the other hand, referred to the physical action they needed to take. Literally, God said, "Move on," meaning just what it says, to stop whining and get going. Moses had not lifted his hands yet to make a path through the sea, but God wanted the Israelites to respond in faith, to take that next step into the water, trusting that God would make a path for them.

All the people knew was what God, through Moses, had told them; but this was enough. They knew he would deliver them and that the Egyptian army would be destroyed. What God needed from them was not more questions, words, skepticism, and doubt—but action. He needed them to move on.

That is God's word to us today as well. When plagued by doubts and the skeletons from your past, move on. When paralyzed by fear and the uncertainty of the future, move on. When your limited vision only allows you to see what lies just ahead, move on. Even when what lies just ahead is a seemingly insurmountable obstacle, move on. Walk as far as you can and trust God for the next step and the step after that.

Think of it this way: it is easier for God to guide us when we are moving than when we are dead weight, standing still. Have you ever tried to move the steering wheel of a car that is not moving? Even with power steering, trying to alter the direction of a motionless vehicle is a challenge because the friction from the rubber against the pavement resists your guidance from the steering wheel. On the other hand, when the vehicle is in motion, you can steer the car with your pinkie finger. I wouldn't recommend this as a rule, but you can do it.

Vehicles were designed to be steered on the go. Likewise, people were created by God to be guided while on the move. As you are going, as you are navigating the next step in your future, God is shining his light on the next step in the path. I wrote earlier of how Proverbs 3:5–6 has been a guiding verse for my family. God will make our paths straight if we trust him. Another of my favorite passages of Scripture is Psalm 119:105, "Your word is a lamp to my feet and a light for my path."

One reason I like this verse so much is the word picture it gives of walking along a path being guided by a lamp or a lantern. If you've ever done this, you know that a lantern does not provide much forward light. It only illuminates the area right around you, providing enough light to see one or two steps ahead.

This is a picture of someone who walks with the Lord. This is a person who trusts Christ to shine the light of his Word just far enough for the next step. It would be easy if we had a detailed itinerary of future events. God does give us a glimpse into the future with prophecy, but he tells us just enough so we can trust him with the future. We know the path will eventually take us home, but in the meantime we have to follow the path each day just as far as God's light will carry us.

DON'T DEIFY FEAR

Trusting God with our future is easier said than done because fear has a way of appearing more powerful than God himself. When we are overwhelmed by a certain situation or with indecision about which way to go, we lose sight of the awesomeness of God. In other words, we make more out of fear than it really is. Fear rather than the power, promise, and provision of God becomes our motivator.

But God gives us direction in his Word on how to put fear in its proper place through the life of an Old Testament man of prayer named Nehemiah. A Jewish man born into Persian captivity, Nehemiah was elevated to the second most important position in the kingdom: wine taster to King Artaxerxes.

Wine tasters back then wielded a lot of power. They would taste the king's wine and taste his food before he ate and drank. If the king saw the wine taster keel over, he knew that the food was tainted or poisoned. But the wine taster was also the king's confidant. He was a trusted advisor with whom the king shared both intimate and state secrets.

One day Nehemiah, a great man of prayer, was praying. God began to tell him to go ask King Artaxerxes for a favor. God wanted him to leave his good job, travel eight hundred miles, and rebuild the city walls around Jerusalem, Nehemiah's home. This was a scary proposition, because Nehemiah had to have the king's permission to leave and carry out this task. If the king didn't like the request, he could be executed.

Nehemiah approached the king with his request. We find the account in Nehemiah 2:

> In the month of Nisan in the twentieth year of King
> Artaxerxes, when wine was brought for him, I took the
> wine and gave it to the king. I had not been sad in his
> presence before; so the king asked me, "Why does your
> face look so sad when you are not ill? This can be nothing
> but sadness of heart."
>
> *I was very much afraid,* but I said to the king, "May
> the king live forever! Why should my face not look sad
> when the city where my fathers are buried lies in ruins,
> and its gates have been destroyed by fire?" (Neh. 2:1–3,
> emphasis added)

Look at Nehemiah's honesty in verse 2 as he recounted this interchange with the king: "I was very much afraid." That is vulnerability and authenticity, the ability to admit one's fear. God often will use fear in our lives to drive us to him, but if we never recognize and admit it, we will not rely on him.

Nehemiah had prayed to God, and now in the midst of his fear, he trusted God with the outcome. Without that sense of fear, he might have tried to confront the king in his own power and strength. But God used this fear to bring Nehemiah to a place of dependence on him. Nehemiah knew he had to have this difficult conversation with the king, but the outcome was completely up to the grace of God.

Nehemiah followed the *admit-commit* rule. He admitted his fear, and he committed it to God in prayer. He talked to God about it in Nehemiah 1:11: "O Lord, let your ear be attentive to the prayer of this your servant and to the prayer of your servants who delight in revering your name. Give your servant success today by granting him favor in the presence of this man." He was still fearful, even after his prayer, because he was still a man with natural emotions. But he committed his anxiety to God and trusted him for the rest.

Then, finally, Nehemiah faced his fear. He walked into the king's palatial office and made the request of King Artaxerxes. Look again in Nehemiah 2:1–3 at what God did. God understood Nehemiah's fears and used those emotions in a positive way. God allowed the king to see the distress on Nehemiah's face, and the king actually asked him why he looked so distraught. The great king of Persia was concerned about the emotional state of his wine taster. This provided an open door for Nehemiah to explain why he looked sad and how the king could help him.

Through Artaxerxes, God granted Nehemiah the privilege of going back and rebuilding the city walls around Jerusalem—and the king of Persia picked up the tab! Nehemiah committed his fears to God, allowing them to be used for his glory, and Artaxerxes financed the entire building project. What an incredible success story!

Nehemiah didn't deify fear and put it on a pedestal. Nehemiah did not bow down to his fear, cower in front of it, or let it rule his life. He admitted it, committed it, and faced it.

Talk to God about your fears instead of deifying them by admitting, "God, I am fearful, but I want you to use me. Help me take a step in the right direction, God." Who is the King Artaxerxes in your life? What fear in your life do you need to face? God is looking for honesty and a willingness to take the first step of faith; he will take care of the rest.

When I was a child, my younger brother and I had our bedrooms upstairs. I have always been bigger than my brother. At that stage of my life, I was a head taller and thirty pounds heavier. But I would never go upstairs at night unless Ben went up first because I was scared of the "little man." I thought a little man lived upstairs in the attic. I pictured him in the bathroom, and I imagined that he was hiding out under my bed.

One night Ben wasn't home. Bedtime rolled around and my parents said, "OK, Ed, it's time to go upstairs." I just stood there in the grip of my private fear.

They said again, "Ed, go upstairs. Go to bed."

"I'm waiting for Ben," I said, looking down at the carpet and shifting my feet nervously.

At this point I knew I had to admit what was going on or risk punishment for defying my parents. So I said quietly, "I'm scared of the little man."

I explained my fears to my mom and dad. I told them about my imaginary "little man" and of all the places I thought he could be hiding. They went upstairs with me and turned on all the lights.

Room by room they helped me face my fear of the boogeyman. We went in the attic and looked around all the boxes. We checked out the bathroom and looked under the bed.

"Ed," they said, "there is no little man up here." My parents had guided me through the house, exposing the darkness to light and helping my fears to fade.

Psalm 27:1 says, "The LORD is my light and my salvation—whom shall I fear? The LORD is the stronghold of my life—of whom shall I be afraid?" Is there a boogeyman in your life that is keeping you from doing something that you know God wants you to do or from going somewhere God wants you to go? When you admit your fear, commit your fear to God, and face your fear together with him, he will put your fear in its proper perspective. When revealed in the light of God and his truth, it will be exposed as nothing more than that imaginary "little man." Don't make fear more than it is. Every fear, regardless of how terrifying it may seem at first, begins to fade when exposed to the light.

STAY AWAY FROM SCENARIO SICKNESS

Have you been assaulted by the flu in the past year? I generally don't get sick very often, but when I do, it can really put me down for the count. I was speaking one week, and in the middle of the message I could feel the flu coming on. I know nothing about medicine: all I know is that to avoid getting sick, you should wash your hands frequently. I washed my hands nonstop, but my efforts at extra cleanliness ended up being too little too late. I was sick for two days, and then the rest of my family got sick as well.

Flu can really mess your system up, but there is an even more severe strain of sickness going around. It's an illness caused by the debilitating effects of fear, and it's called "scenario sickness." This disease is highly contagious, and the symptoms are severe. It will tie you up in fear and keep you from being all that God wants you to be. But you can guard against this dreaded disease in the same way that I tried to avoid the flu: you have to wash. In this case, unlike the flu virus, washing is a sure-fire way of staying away from the fearsome contagion that causes scenario sickness.

Psalm 51:2 shares the remedy for this sickness: "Wash away all my iniquity and cleanse me from my sin." The word *iniquity* is another word for sin, for falling short of the mark of God's glory, his perfect character. Like it or not, scenario sickness is a sin before God. Although it's a very common part of the human condition, it is still an affront to God. Because it keeps us from being all that God wants us to be, we must deal with it by asking God to wash us, to cleanse us from those sins that have brought on the illness.

Here is what happens with someone who has a bad case of scenario sickness. Because of ever-present fearful emotions, this person constantly runs over all the scenarios in his mind of why he can't do what God wants him to do. He constantly rationalizes his lack of action with what-if scenarios, "What might happen if I do this? What if that happens?" A cloud of pessimism hangs over his head, and he lives in fear of the worst possible thing happening for any and every situation. It's the epitome of a self-defeating outlook on life.

When I think of the person with scenario sickness, I am reminded of Charles Schultz's comic strip character, Charlie Brown. In one particular Charlie Brown special, *A Charlie Brown Christmas*, Charlie goes to Lucy's corner stand for psychiatric advice. The sign on her stand says, "Psychiatric Advice: 5 cents."

Charlie pays his nickel and then tells her that he should feel happy but he doesn't and he doesn't know why. Lucy proceeds to review a list of fears and phobias to find out if Charlie Brown suffers from any of them. Finally she says, "Maybe you have a fear of everything."

Charlie responds, "That's it! I'm afraid of everything."

This is the common symptom of the person with scenario sickness. He is afraid of everything and is certain that, no matter what he does, it will turn out wrong. He responds to this all-encompassing fear by not trying anything new.

People who have this sickness also tend to hang out together. They are like the Israelites: whining and moaning, fearful, paralyzed, and tyrannized. They don't care about commitment. They are lonely. They are afraid of stepping out. They are even afraid of God and death. In short, they are stricken with fear. Their future looks bleak, no matter how you slice it.

STEP OUT BOLDLY

Instead of coming down with a case of scenario sickness, we need to take our cue from a defining event in the life of Miriam, the oldest sister of Moses, in the life of Moses himself, and, ultimately, in the life of the Jewish people.

First, let me set up the background of this important event. The Israelites had been under the yoke of slavery in Egypt for hundreds of years, and they were increasing greatly in numbers. They had grown as a people to such a degree that Pharaoh feared their power and ability to revolt against oppression. As a result, he gave an order that all male Hebrew infants must be thrown into the Nile River. It was during this time that Moses was born.

Moses' mother hid him for three months, but she could hide him no longer. Not wanting to drown him, as the law required, she and her daughter Miriam made a floating bassinet. They put Moses in the bassinet, placed it in the river, and pushed him along the muddy waters of the Nile.

The Bible says that Miriam stood in the distance and watched as her brother Moses drifted downstream. The timing was perfect, because she knew Pharaoh's daughter was coming to the river to bathe. When Pharaoh's daughter took baby Moses out of the Nile, Miriam walked up to her. "Have I got a deal for you! You need a nurse for the baby, and I know someone who would be perfect." Pharaoh's daughter ended up paying Miriam and her mother to take care of her own son, and the family was reunited.

Miriam did not have scenario sickness. What if she had played all the possible outcomes in her mind over and over again? "Oh, what if I say the wrong thing to Pharaoh's daughter? What if she doesn't like my idea? Oh, no, I'm so fearful!" She didn't do that; she boldly went into the situation and did what she needed to do. God used Miriam to deliver the deliverer Moses into the hands of Pharaoh's daughter, who would preserve his life until he could fulfill his place in Israel's history.

Because Miriam stepped out boldly, because she seized the opportunity that presented itself and took action even in the face of what must have been a very fearful situation, Moses' life was spared and God's chosen people were freed from oppression. We do not know what might have happened if Miriam had been paralyzed by fear, if she had let the negative scenarios keep her from taking action at just the right time. God could have saved Moses by some other means, but only he knows what might have happened if Miriam had not stepped up to the challenge.

We have to realize that God has a plan for each of our lives. When we let what-if scenarios scare us away from fulfilling God's plan, there is no way to know how that will affect the future. We cannot know what chain of events is set in motion by our lack of action. God's plan for mankind will be accomplished regardless of how we act or react to the opportunities we are given, but in some mysterious way God allows us to participate in his plan. And our action or lack of action somehow makes a difference in the quality of the outcome.

I will admit that over the years there have been times when I was hesitant to take a bold step for God. I can think of several times, particularly, in the history of Fellowship Church where I have been, quite frankly, a little overwhelmed by the responsibilities God placed on me. One particular time a few years ago comes to mind when I felt an unusually high amount of anxiety about the present circumstances as well as the uncertainty of the future.

Fellowship Church was experiencing a huge growth spurt, we were in rented facilities, and we were at a point where we had to begin to step out in faith for the future ministry of the church. The logistics of running the ministry at our current location were taxing all of our staff, volunteers, resources, and space to the max. We were trying some creative things to accommodate for the growth, some of which were working and some were not. And at the rate we were growing, even with plans to purchase land and build permanent facilities, we were looking at several more years of cramped quarters and logistical headaches.

The decisions that the leaders of the church were having to make involved large amounts of money, major planning, and strategic efforts. This was a time that tested my faith as a senior pastor, the faith of our leadership, and the faith of our church members in a great way. If you have been through a process like this, you know what I am talking about. And throughout this process of making plans for the future, my anxiety began to build. I began to wonder how we were going to accomplish and sustain this great task as we prepared for a church that could minister to thousands of people each week.

I began to wonder if God was really asking us to take this bold step of faith. I wondered if perhaps we were misinterpreting his leading and trying to go too far too fast. If we made by faith the kind of financial and resource commitments we were planning, would God bless our show of faith? Or were we just rushing headlong into disaster? All of these questions flooded my mind and heart. It was a time of great anxiety for me but also a time of great growth.

We did as a church step out boldly in faith. I had been walking with Christ long enough to know not to trust my feelings but to consider prayerfully all of the signs and assurances that God gives along the way. And God did give me and the other leaders of the church many assurances that we were going in the right direction. You can take a look at our Web site and read through our history to get an idea of how God has led us over the years.

But I learned through that experience, and through many others since then in my life and ministry, that God only reveals his plan to us one step at a time. And that first step can be a doozy, believe me. With every step, though, we grow stronger and more confident that we are following God's will and that he will carry our work to completion. I say now and have always said that the ministry of Fellowship Church is a God thing. I pray that you can experience the joy of being a part of some incredible "God things" in your life as you step out boldly for him.

God gives us both the responsibility and the privilege of taking part in his work; and I have to believe that what we do makes a difference. God is sovereign; he is in control of everything, but we are also free beings with the capacity to make choices. And those choices affect the course of our lives and those of other people. Make the choice to be bold in your work for the Lord. Keep scenario sickness from striking by confessing negativism as sin and making bold moves for God as he leads you.

RIDE THE ROLLER COASTER

As we begin to make bold choices in our lives, we need to realize that life will be exciting. Sometimes it will seem beyond our control, and often it will be. God will be in control, and, as the apostle Paul tells us, his strength will be made perfect in our weakness. Rest assured that life will always promise to be an exciting ride. Adventure and excitement are the essence of the Christian life.

There is nothing boring about being a Christian, unless you are paralyzed by fear and take the easy road. But God has not called us to the easy road; he has called us to the narrow road, a road filled with ups and downs, hills and valleys, and many tight curves and bends. This is the great adventure of following Christ, the roller coaster of a life of authentic faith. There is no place for worry or timidity in the kind of life God wants us to have.

The movie *Parenthood*, starring Steve Martin and Mary Steenburgen, takes a poignant look at the contrast between a life of worry and a life of boldness. I need to warn you that this movie takes a candid look at the struggles of parenting today, so it does have some rough content. I am not recommending this movie for family viewing, so no cards, letters, or phone calls, please.

While the story line does not come necessarily from a Christian point of view, I appreciate one of its underlying messages. It emphasizes the debilitating effects of fear and anxiety in our lives. This is a movie about life in general, not specifically the Christian life, but it speaks well of the need to embrace the adventure and excitement in life with all of its ups and downs.

Steve Martin plays a worried father named Gil Buckman, who is raising a son just like him. Gil grew up with a furrow in his brow and a knot in his stomach. He can't seem to enjoy life because there is always a black cloud above every silver lining. Likewise, Gil's son Kevin seems to have the cares of the whole world on his shoulders, and his emotional problems are such that he requires psychiatric therapy.

Kevin worries about what kids think of him and lives in constant fear of messing up at school, in Little League games, at birthday parties—and the list goes on. His fears keep him from stepping out and trying new things, and they cause emotional problems and even physical symptoms, such as stomach aches.

At one point near the end of the film, Gil is speaking to his wife, played by Steenburgen, about Kevin's success earlier that day in the Little League baseball game. He comments that, in light of all the other things going on in their lives, it seems wrong for him to be so excited about the pop fly that Kevin caught that day. In the midst of his problems at work, his wife's pregnancy (their fourth) with an unplanned child, and their son's academic and emotional problems, Gil finds a moment of joy in Kevin's success on the baseball field.

He says to her, "Doesn't it seem perverse that a father can get so much pleasure out of his son catching a pop fly?"

He then goes through a bout of scenario sickness, throwing out a string of what-ifs. "What if he hadn't caught that ball?"

She responds, "But he did."

"But what if he didn't?"

"Well, he did," she responds irritably, pointing out that he narrowed the odds considerably by throwing about a million pop flies to him in the backyard.

She doesn't understand the dilemma. Why shouldn't he be happy? She doesn't have the same outlook on life as her husband but takes each moment as it comes. She experiences the joy or sorrow of each moment, however it presents itself. Gil wraps all of his past worries and future worries together and feels guilty for these little moments of pleasure. How can he feel good about his son catching a ball when there are so many big things to worry about?

Gil's grandmother enters the room at this point and begins to tell a story about a roller coaster that she once rode with her husband long ago and how much she enjoyed the ride.

Gil makes some sarcastic comment about the irrelevance of her little story. And his wife says, "I think your grandmother is brilliant. I happen to like roller coasters."

What is going on here? This exchange presents a fundamental difference between outlooks on life. Gil sees every curve, hill, and dip ahead in the tracks and worries about what might happen. His wife and his grandmother have learned to enjoy each moment for what it's worth.

Sometimes, even in the midst of painful or stressful times, we are given the gift of joy in the little things of life. Our son or daughter makes a nice catch at the Little League game. The sun shines after a long rain. A moment of laughter breaks a long period of tension. You hear the words "I love you" at just the right time from someone you love and say them in return.

You begin to realize that tomorrow has enough problems of its own and the past is past, so it is all right to enjoy God's present of the present. With each little joy that suddenly opens up to you, your brow begins to unfurrow and the knot in the pit of your stomach begins to unwind.

The movie ends with a wonderful scene at their daughter's school play, where their youngest son wanders on stage and causes a domino effect of destruction and mayhem. As the sets and props begin to topple over and the play deteriorates to a state of chaos, Gil's stomach tightens again.

You can see the distress on his face as the entire audience rises to its feet in reaction to the chaotic situation. Some are yelling at him; others are laughing. The roller coaster is moving again. The car is careening around curves and up and down the precipitous track. But it is obvious that Gil is not enjoying the ride.

Until he looks over at his wife's sweet face. She has a grin from ear to ear and is even laughing. She watches with amazement, wonder, and amusement as her son, quite literally, brings down the house in that elementary school auditorium. There is, at last, a sign of recognition on Gil's face. This is the roller coaster. Stop worrying and enjoy the ride.

Jesus summarized the appropriate response to worry and anxiety in Matthew 6:34: "Therefore do not worry about tomorrow, for tomorrow will worry about itself. Each day has enough trouble of its own." Every time you read the word *therefore,* ask yourself what it is there for. It means Jesus is going to say something strong. This verse says that worry and anxiety are sins before God. The word *worry* literally means to be pulled in different directions. Are you being pulled in different directions? Or are you focused on the opportunities and challenges that God has given you today, just today?

We're incredible spin doctors regarding worry. We don't call it "worry" any more. We say, "I am maxed out," or, "I'm feeling stressed." Many of us are so worried about tomorrow that it messes us up for today. This causes a chain reaction of worry and stress, resulting in a messed-up tomorrow. And this cycle goes on and on until we don't know anything else in our lives but a constant feeling of worry and anxiety.

Jesus is telling us in Matthew 6:34 to break free from this cycle by finding a center of peace and contentment in the plans and purposes of God. God knows your tomorrows. Take care of God's plan for your life today, and trust in his plans for all of your tomorrows. When you yield to his control and trust the future to him, you have found the antidote for future fears. Instead of being pulled in a myriad of directions, you are allowing yourself to be pulled in only one direction—God's direction.

Do a quick relational inventory. Are you rubbing shoulders with people who have scenario sickness? If you are, do some washing. Break away and say, "God, I want to meet a Moses. I want to meet a Nehemiah. I want to meet a Miriam. I want fearless people to surround and befriend me, so I can replace my fears of the future with an assurance of your plans and purposes for my life."

Facing Life's Phobias

STAND FIRM

- "Do not be afraid. Stand firm and you will see the deliverance the LORD will bring you today. The Egyptians you see today you will never see again. The LORD will fight for you; you need only to be still" (Exod. 14:13–14).
- "Be still, and know that I am God" (Ps. 46:10).

TAKE THE NEXT STEP

- Then the LORD said to Moses, "Why are you crying out to me? Tell the Israelites to move on. Raise your staff and stretch out your hand over the sea to divide the water so that the Israelites can go through the sea on dry ground" (Exod. 14:15–16).
- Your word is a lamp to my feet and a light for my path (Ps. 119:105).

DON'T DEIFY FEAR

- I was very much afraid, but I said to the king, "May the king live forever! Why should my face not look sad when the city where my fathers are buried lies in ruins, and its gates have been destroyed by fire?" (Neh. 2:2b–3).
- "O Lord, let your ear be attentive to the prayer of this your servant and to the prayer of your servants who delight in

revering your name. Give your servant success today by granting him favor in the presence of this man" (Neh. 1:11).

- The LORD is my light and my salvation—whom shall I fear? The LORD is the stronghold of my life—of whom shall I be afraid? (Ps. 27:1).

STAY AWAY FROM SCENARIO SICKNESS

- Wash away all my iniquity and cleanse me from my sin (Ps. 51:2).

STEP OUT BOLDLY

- His sister stood at a distance to see what would happen to him (Exod. 2:4).
- Then his sister asked Pharaoh's daughter, "Shall I go and get one of the Hebrew women to nurse the baby for you?" "Yes, go," she answered. And the girl went and got the baby's mother (Exod. 2:7–8).

RIDE THE ROLLER COASTER

- "Therefore do not worry about tomorrow, for tomorrow will worry about itself. Each day has enough trouble of its own" (Matt. 6:34).

STEPPING OUT

Fear of Commitment

We'd rather bail out than blast through. We'd rather leave than last. We'd rather throw in the towel than stay in the game. It's so easy to waver and waffle and take the path of least resistance. Why? Because we fear this ten-letter word that symbolizes accountability, integrity, and discipline: commitment.

From month-to-month apartment leases to prenuptial agreements, from playing career hopscotch to escape clauses, our culture is characterized by a lack of or fear of commitment. "I don't want to be hemmed in," we declare. "I want to keep my options open. I don't want to be stifled or handcuffed."

Commitment means pledging yourself to a position no matter the price tag, pledging yourself to a stance no matter what the cost. And if you make the effort to invest in commitment, the returns will be awesome.

I live in the heart of the Dallas-Fort Worth area, which means that—to put it mildly—the Cowboys are big. When my son EJ was eight, I decided he was ready for his first Cowboys game. In Dallas, this is the ultimate father-son bonding experience. I was pumped. And EJ was, if possible, even more excited.

We found our seats and waited expectantly for the big kickoff. EJ passed the time by sampling the wares of every vendor within a fifty-foot radius, deciding that whatever they were selling was vital to his enjoyment of the game. Finally, the Giants kicked off to the Cowboys, and they returned the ball all the way to the Giants' six-yard line. The fans were going ballistic. They were on their feet, jumping up and down, high-fiving, yelling, "How 'bout them Cowboys!" as though they expected an answer.

Unfortunately, three short downs later the Cowboys still had not scored. They had failed to put the expected six points on the board. And then, to my amazement, a chorus of boos rang out from around the sixty-thousand-seat stadium.

I looked around and began to laugh. Thousands of so-called "fans" were blaming everyone they could think of: the refs, the coaching staff, and the players—who had all forgotten more about the game in a week than these fickle football followers would ever know. The ones making the most noise were the overweight, beer-drinking baby boomers who couldn't outrun the coach much less play a down of football.

Then to top it all off, in the midst of the booing, the Cowboys' kicker trotted onto the field and kicked a field goal. EJ looked at the scoreboard: Cowboys 3, Giants 0. Against the backdrop of all the boos, EJ looked up at me with a huge grin and said, "Yeah, the Cowboys scored! We've got three, Dad! Isn't that great?"

As I looked back at him, smiling, I could see all the fair-weather fans booing behind him. Even when the Cowboys were stumbling and fumbling, EJ was committed: he had pledged himself to a position, no matter what.

Too often, we are fair-weather fans of the game of life. Things are going well for us. We're making money, the stock market is up, the marriage is going well. Our relationships are just sailing along, and we look committed. We say, "Yeah, how about my life! How about my career!" Then we get a couple of losses under our belt, the economy goes south, we lose our number one client, and we have a conflict. When that happens, we greet the whole situation with a chorus of boos. Because we are not really committed for the long haul, a few setbacks threaten to derail us.

WHY DON'T WE COMMIT?

Why do we struggle with and fear commitment? Some of us fear commitment because we have been rejected. We have put our heart and soul into something and had it trashed, so we are apprehensive about putting it out there again.

Others of us have had an authority figure—perhaps a parent or teacher or coach—commit to us and then fall through on their promise. Maybe they said they were going to show up, take us to the game or fishing or shopping, and they didn't keep their word. We remember the hurt of those experiences and fear going through the same thing again.

Yet another group of us fears commitment because we have broken so many promises ourselves. We don't like to dwell on those failures, so we say, "Why think about it? Why talk about it? Why make commitments if I can't ever follow through on the promises I make?"

All of these things lead to a fear of commitment, but our true fear can be traced all the way back to the soil of the Garden of Eden. The Bible says that God was committed to Adam and Eve. He showed his hand, put his cards on the table. Adam and Eve recognized this, and they, in turn, were committed to God. When God said, "Adam, Eve, don't touch the fruit of the tree in the middle of the garden," they responded with, "Lord, we are committed to that. We want to obey you. We want to follow you. We want to be your people."

Satan always attacks our commitment. If you do a quick background check on him, you'll discover that he always struggled with commitment himself. When he was in heaven as Lucifer, he struggled with staying committed to God and got kicked out. From that day forward, he has been trying to tear apart your commitment and mine.

So Satan attacked Adam and Eve. He said, "Hey, guys, God is holding out on you. If you eat of the fruit of the tree, you will become like God. Don't really commit to him. For once, just back off. For once, just bail out. For once, just leave." Adam and Eve tried it. They blew their commitment and failed the test, and from that day forward we have been struggling with this issue.

Too Legit to Quit

Psalm 37:5 (NASB) reads, "Commit your way to the LORD, Trust also in Him, and He will do it." What a promise and an assurance! First Kings 8:61 tells us, "But your hearts must be fully committed to the LORD our God, to live by his decrees and obey his commands, as at this time." Notice the phrase "at this time."

One of our six-year-old twins asked my wife Lisa, "Mommy, when will it be the year 1999 again?"

Lisa replied, "Landra, it will never be 1999 again."

It's the truth. Now is the only time you have for sure to commit. Yesterday is gone and tomorrow is uncertain. Do it now. You can't bring back 1999, 1998, or any other time in your life, but you can commit yourself to God right now, today.

I want to give you a crash course on commitment. There are ways we can commit to God. If we follow through on these ways, he will increase our level of commitment and give us incredible returns.

SHIFT INTO FOUR-WHEEL DRIVE

I used to drive a pickup truck with four-wheel drive. I didn't use the four-wheel drive feature very much, but now and then it helped me out. I knew that if I got into an off-road situation, I could shift into four-wheel drive to get out.

Marriage is wonderful, the most important earthly relationship we will ever have. But I would be lying to you if I said that marriage was a cruise control or Autobahn situation. If you are married, you have off-road moments. You can't just cruise down the road at full speed and never expect to encounter bumps in the road. You have to slow down from time to time or pull aside and take an off-road detour.

Lisa and I have had our off-road moments, days, weeks, and years. We have had them in the past, and we will have them in the future. When you hit a sticking point and you have a problem, it is as though you have suddenly veered off the smooth freeway and started off-roading. Mud is slinging; you are burning up fuel. But if you are committed, totally committed, if you have pledged yourself to a position, no matter what, you will shift into four-wheel drive and get through the off-road situation. You will burst through it and build deeper levels of commitment, love, and intimacy.

Here, though, is the problem. When husbands and wives hit some off-road situations or when it gets a little dicey and the vehicle starts to spin, they just bail out. They ditch the car and say, "I'm going to find another one. I need to get into another relationship, another marriage." Little do they realize that they will hit the same off-road patches in the next marriage, and the next, and the next.

If you are not willing to four-wheel-drive it, then, to put it bluntly, do not get married. Trust me, it will save you a lot of pain and heartache if you will assess your level of commitment now and back off. This is better than getting into the thick of the relationship and realizing that you never had the commitment level you needed to stick it out, to commit for the long haul.

What separates great marriages from mediocre ones? Great marriages are willing to go four-wheeling and crash through the off-road times, because both partners know it is worth it when they do it God's way. Sadly, most husbands and wives wait too long to say one little word that can change the course of their marriage: Help! When the vehicle is stuck and the wheels are spinning, instead of saying, "Help!" they just sit there and resign themselves to being stuck.

Too many give up too soon and do not take advantage of the resources available to help them through the rough times. "Yeah, we've been married for twelve years and we are still married. We're sitting here in this four-wheel-drive vehicle, but we don't really want to engage the power of the four-wheel drive system. We are just stuck, we can't move, we're broken down." If only they would seek a great Christian friend, a pastor, or a Christian counselor who could help them engage the four-wheel drive and get them out of the mud.

If you were driving home from work and you had some car trouble, would you just sit there on the side of the road for a couple of years? No, you'd get proactive: you would get on your cell phone and do something. If you are in a marriage relationship that is stuck in the mud with your tires spinning, do something. Get help. Be committed and say, "We're going to work it out. We're going to make it happen. We're going to do it God's way."

You also have to be willing to shift into four-wheel drive with your children. Moms and dads these days say, "We want to bring up kids who are committed, kids who pledge themselves to a position, no matter what." Parents say that, yet they go back on their word. They sign up but don't show up. They say that, yet they let a couple of raindrops keep them from church. They expect their children to be committed, but parents need to know that children scoop up commitment cues from the committed behavior—not just the words—of Mom and Dad. They are taking it all in, watching us. We are always on stage in the family theater, and the spotlight never goes dim.

Be committed to spending time with your children, both quantity time and quality time. You may rationalize the lack of time you spend with your children by saying, "I may not have a lot of time to give, but I spend quality time with my kids." That's a fallacy. Kids do not understand this concept, and, quite frankly, it is just an excuse to make parents feel better about their misplaced priorities and lack of commitment. Quality time emerges from quantity time. You can't put those special moments with your children in a

Daytimer or a Palm Pilot. Those special moments emerge spontaneously from spending time—quantities of time—with them.

This commitment to our children includes quality conversation. It means really listening to them, even when the content of their conversation seems trivial to us. It's not trivial to them. Make eye contact with them and communicate that their presence is important to you. If you listen to them when they are five, they will talk to you when they are fifteen and twenty-five.

Make sure, moms and dads, that you are committed to introducing your children to an intimate and vibrant relationship with the Lord, Jesus Christ. Teach them how to pray. Teach them how to read the Bible. Make sure you have them in a church that offers age-appropriate teaching for preschoolers, children, and students.

Your kids will often struggle against going to church. You know this will happen, but it should not keep you from taking charge and doing what you know is the right thing for the spiritual welfare of your children. They may say, "I don't want to go. It's not my thing. None of my friends will be there." You know, it might be a growing experience that their regular friends are not there. They will make new friends from families that are also committed to making church a priority in their lives. Parents, this is an off-road stretch where you need to shift into four-wheel drive. I want to ask you a basic question: Who is in the driver's seat? Are you driving, or have you given your children the keys?

My parents are human and far from perfect, but they are pretty much three for three as far as their three boys are concerned. My two brothers and I have had long, vibrant relationships with Christ. We never went through the dope-smoking, cocaine-snorting, women-chasing, beer-drinking, hell-raising stage that a lot of people go through. God has given me an incredible ministry at Fellowship Church in Grapevine, Texas, along with a nationally syndicated radio program and the privilege of sharing my teaching in books like this. My middle brother, Ben, is the pastor of one of the nation's largest singles' ministries at Second Baptist Church in Houston, Texas. He has a nationally syndicated Christian radio talk show for single adults and has written several books. And my youngest brother, Cliff, is in a contemporary Christian band, Caedmon's Call, that is rapidly rising in the charts.

Now let me assure you that we are not perfect. All three of us have messed up many times—but we have stayed the course, because our parents were willing to four-wheel drive it. They would listen when I complained about going to church and respond, "Ed, we appreciate that. We hear you, but jump in the car, baby, because we're going to church today."

The fact that my dad has been a pastor for many years notwithstanding, church has always been a focal point in our family's life. And, more than that, we were raised in a home that took Christian commitment seriously. Our commitment to the local church was an outgrowth of our commitment to living out biblical principles individually and as a family unit. Christianity is not a one-day proposition. It is a full-time, full-out commitment to the person and teachings of Jesus Christ. Do your family priorities reflect that kind of commitment and dedication to following Christ?

THE BIMBA PRINCIPLE

When I think of family priorities and making God the center of family life, I can't help but mention the apostle Paul's warning in

2 Corinthians about being unequally yoked. If both partners are not committed to the things of God growing out of a vibrant relationship with Jesus Christ, then trying to make Christ the center of family life will be even more of an uphill struggle than it already is.

So let me warn you now, if you are a Christian single contemplating a marriage relationship with an unbeliever—please take this to heart—you are in for some serious heartache and misery. Just do not go there. I can't say it more forcefully than that. God has given us this warning because of the kind of struggles that will inevitably follow if you try to build a marriage and a family with an unbelieving spouse.

I have some friends who live in Cancún, Quintana Roo, Mexico. I visited them years ago, and they had a pet monkey that really took a liking to me. Monkeys are strong, and have a tenacious grip. Bimba would hold on to me all day and let me carry her around everywhere. But if I wanted to put her down, good luck. She would dig in her nails and wrap her tail around me. Bimba was going to hold on to me, no matter what.

Singles, you have to remember the Bimba principle: Hold on tight to God's teaching concerning spouse selection. Don't let go of one very important principle from Scripture that speaks directly to choosing your life partner because God gives this to us for our own good. Paul says in 2 Corinthians 6:14 (NASB), "Do not be bound together with unbelievers; for what partnership have righteousness and lawlessness, or what fellowship has light with darkness?"

What is going on here? Is God being discriminatory? No. Is God saying that we should never have friends outside the family of God? No. Is he insisting that our best friends and the people we date have the same spiritual intensity as we do? Emphatically, yes! He is saying that the people we are closest to must share the same treasure that we share.

Why would God say this, specifically in the dating area? When you are dating, you are really thinking about finding a mate. I don't care how casual the date is; you are thinking about getting married: Could this be the one? Could this be him? Could this be her? God insists on this rule because he wants us to share ultimate intimacy. He knows how terrible it would be for us to be hooked up to someone with whom we couldn't share the most important thing in our life.

God also insists on this because he knows we will need his help when we get into an off-road situation. When both parties know him personally, they can draw on a common power source when the tires are spinning and the mud is slinging. I have talked to many, many couples where one is a Christ-follower and the other is not. They are going in different directions. One partner is tapping into God's source, and the other is tapping into something else. In short, they have some serious problems with focus and priorities in their marriage and family.

God also wants us to have spiritual compatibility because of the challenges of child-rearing. If we share him, we will operate from the same foundation, the same authority, and the same absolutes when we are rearing children. Both parents will be unified in saying, "Hey, we are going to church. Hey, you are going to the junior high or high school ministry." If one parent is urging the child to think of the things of God and the other is saying, "Come on, honey, it doesn't matter; just let the kid do what he wants," you are in for a lot of pain and anguish.

Single females, in particular, tend to go through an interesting transition. When they are young, they say, "OK, I am going to commit to the Bimba principle. I am going to hold on. I'm going to do it God's way." Then one day they suddenly realize that the biological clock is ticking, and they begin to change. Their standard of finding and marrying a man who is committed to Christ and his principles has degenerated into, "Well, if he shaves and wears pants, that is good enough for me. I can change him; I can tweak him. He'll come around eventually."

If you are a single man reading this and laughing, hold on. Don't laugh too soon, because men aren't any better in the realm of commitment than their female counterparts. Here is what guys tend to do when faced with commitment. Too many Christian guys get right on the edge of a committed relationship and bail out. They have a good relationship with a great Christian girl, and they know that pretty soon they are going to have to take the next step. But they freak out and begin to waffle and waver: "Wow, if I got married, I would have to be responsible! I couldn't play in thirteen softball leagues at once! I know she loves the Lord, but what if Tyra Banks came to know Christ personally and I ran into her one day?"

Guys, we are pretty stupid. It's important to be attracted to the person you date and the person you marry. But if you always say, "Well, I'm waiting for someone better-looking," you will never get anywhere. God wants you to look, as he does, first at the heart, not the body. Marriage is a step of faith, a step of commitment, to that one person with whom you can partner for life in service to the Lord. Outward beauty will fade, and the body will begin to give way, but the spiritual strength of your relationship together will last forever.

The bottom line is that you have to pledge yourself to a position, no matter what. And the first commitment should be to determine to follow God's principle of not being unequally yoked. Don't let your emotions or your lusts win the day on this one.

I wrote a little book about a year ago entitled *The Ulti-Mate: Finding the Love of Your Life,* primarily for the singles in my church. In it I elaborate more on the principles God has given us regarding dating and finding the ulti-mate for our lives. I want to share a little excerpt from that book with you, because I believe this issue is so vital to the commitment level we have in our marriages, in our families, and in our relationship with God:

I am a why person, always asking why. Why would God set forth these standards? Is God being restrictive? No. God is being protective and He wants the best for you and the best for me. That is why I picked a Mercedes 500SL, a $90,000 sports car, as an illustration. This is one of the best cars made. But in God's economy, your life and mine make this incredible car look like a wreck. That's how much we are loved and the kind of potential we have. God wants to spare us the pain and agony of being unequally yoked, of being hooked up with another human being who does not have the same strength or the same octane or the same RPMs that Christ brings. Why? God wants us to be equally yoked with believers because His desire for us is that we reach our ulti-mate destination.

That is what dating is all about: to find the ulti-mate. I don't care how casual it is. I don't care how flippant it is.

Down deep, I'm talking even to guys now, you are thinking, "Could she be the one? Could she be my wife, the
mother of my children? Could I grow old with her?" And
I know, women, that you are thinking the same kinds of
thoughts about the men you date. Do you want to reach
your ulti-mate destination? Do you want to hit on all
eight cylinders? Then connect with another Christ-
follower. Frankly, my heart is grieved and broken for so
many people who make the wrong call, thinking they can
somehow reach their ulti-mate destination without being
equally yoked. It is a formula for failure.[1]

If you are wondering about my reference to the Mercedes,
throughout *The Ulti-Mate,* I compare the ultimate mate with an
expensive sports car. I do this not to belittle people but because so
many people can identify with the analogy of having a dream car.
And in a similar though much more significant way, we have a
dream person out there whom we want as a mate. God has a dream
person for us as well if we will follow his guidelines for dating and
marriage.

If you are currently in a dating relationship in which you have
doubts about the other person's Christian commitment, take a
step back and allow God to give you discernment. See a counselor
or maybe read a good Christian book that will give you more
insight into God's principles about spouse selection. Marriage is a
lifelong commitment, so be sure you are with someone with
whom you can also share your number one commitment to Jesus
Christ.

RE-LEECH-IONSHIPS

Let's take it down a step further: from marriage to dating, and now to friendships. Just about anyone you ask these days will tell you that close friends are hard to find and even harder to keep. You may be surrounded by people at work, at church, and in the neighborhood, but you don't really have any committed friends.

It would be nice to say that the problem lies with everyone else, but I'm afraid we will have to spread the blame around evenly. As we examine the reasons for a lack of committed friendships in our lives, we need to look first at ourselves for answers to the problem.

Why can't we commit to our friends? What is the problem? We may blame our mobile society or the large size of our churches or our busy schedules, but those really are just surface issues. The problem, I believe, stems from a lack of balance in the way we cultivate and maintain relationships and in the kinds of relationships we foster in our lives. The problem, many times, is that we don't really have relationships; instead, we have *re-leech-ionships*.

If you have ever had a leech attached to your skin, you will have a better understanding of what I am referring to when I use the term *re-leech-ionship*. If you have not had that unpleasant experience, allow me to illustrate. I have a friend named Biff who was a Marine in Vietnam. Biff, the Marine from West Texas, and I, for some unspecified reason, were wading through a swamp one day. We were knee-deep in the muck and mud of this hot, humid swampland. When we got to his car, I took off my soggy socks and shoes and discovered something on my leg.

As I took a closer look at this big, black slimy thing on my calf, I realized what it was. It was a leech. I hate leeches, and I have a greater degree of empathy now for people who were erroneously medically treated with leeches prior to the advances in medical technology in the twentieth century. Anyway, I tried to brush off this black parasite from my leg, but it would not let go. It started to wiggle a little bit, and that is when I began to freak out.

Biff was really on the ball. In a sort of unconcerned tone of voice he said, "Ed, you have a big, ol' leech on you, man. That's a beauty. We used to have those in the jungles of Vietnam. I'll just burn it off for you."

I said, "What?"

He said, "I'll have to burn it off. It's the only way to get it to let go."

Before I knew it, he was holding me down with one hand, with a lighter in the other, and burning the leech off my leg. I have to say it was a horrifying experience that I don't care to repeat. I am not well-versed in medical history, but I can't imagine how intelligent people would ever opt for this as a viable treatment for any sort of disease. I understand, though, that leeches are still used by some practitioners for treating tissue trauma or blood clots. But that is a topic for another sort of book—one that I am not qualified to write.

If you have not figured this out by now, leeches suck blood. They just hang on to you for all they are worth and drain the life out of you. The most popular methods for getting rid of them are either to burn them off or wait for them to have their fill of your blood and subsequently fall off. Though far from pleasant, the burning method, I should think, is preferable to just waiting around for them to fall off. You may know of other solutions, but these are the ones I have most commonly heard used.

What does this have to do with relationships? I repeat, instead of real friendships, a lot of us have *re-leech-ionships:* friendships with people who drain us, who suck our blood, and then leave us dry. I am sorry if that sounds harsh, but if you have been in this type of relationship, you know the description is a valid one. I don't mean to be unkind or uncharitable, but there are people out there who, if we are not careful, will take and take and take and never give back. Because of negative experiences like these, we often shy away from committing to close relationships. We are afraid of repeating the leeching cycle.

These are people who constantly come to us for counsel, who want to spend a lot of time with us so they can download all of their troubles, and who may even want financial or other help from time to time. But when you leave their company, you feel wiped out. They have become more of a ministry to you than a nourishing friendship. And there most certainly is a place for people like that in our lives. We are called by Christ to minister to the needy, to help people and give to people in the name of Christ.

These, however, are not the kind of friends the Bible describes as being closer than a brother. These are friends or acquaintances who need to benefit from you, maybe emotionally or financially, but who are not able to give back in return. The problem with surrounding yourself only with these types of ministry relationships is that, if you have too many re-leech-ionships, you won't have enough energy left over to get into good, replenishing relationships—the kind of solid relationships that hold you accountable and challenge you.

Furthermore, most of us do not have the guts to burn off these relationships when we begin to feel overwhelmed. I would never have had the guts to burn the leech off my leg without the help of my friend Biff. Burning off the leeches in your life does not mean you have to say, "Forget you," and never speak to them again. It means you should turn down the intensity of those relationships that sap your strength and build up the intensity of replenishing, refueling relationships. You must have a balance of both.

You may have times in your life when you need more of one type of relationship than the other. But you must seek out and cultivate on a regular basis friendships that will give you the energy and the strength to carry out the ministry opportunities God gives you. You simply cannot continually minister to others, giving of yourself, without being recharged.

How can you tell the difference between a relationship and a re-leech-ionship? If you are with friends and you find yourself looking at your watch and saying, "Whoa, is it midnight already? I can't believe how fast the time has gone by," that's a replenishing relationship. If you are sharing with them what really makes you tick, your dreams and hopes and fears, and they are doing the same with you, those are replenishing relationships. If you leave them feeling energized and ready to face the world, those are replenishing relationships.

Obviously, the people you call your closest friends should know Christ personally and have the same desire to please him as you do. When you have friends like that, you will soar. Your commitment quotient will increase, and you will have an incredible return on your relational investment.

In re-leech-ionships, on the other hand, you find yourself looking at your watch and saying, "Has it only been thirty minutes? It feels like I've been talking to this guy for hours." You'll be giving away more than you receive because these types of relationships are one-sided. You minister to them, but they have little or nothing to offer to you.

Again, there is a place for these relationships because Christ had relationships like these. Jesus was often so drained by those to whom he ministered that he had to draw away from the crowds and spend time alone with the Father, the ultimate replenishing relationship. Luke records one such experience: "Yet the news about him spread all the more, so that crowds of people came to hear him and to be healed of their sicknesses. But Jesus often withdrew to lonely places and prayed" (Luke 5:15–16). Jesus also spent a lot of time with his disciples, the Twelve with whom he had chosen to interact and share his life. He would draw away with them, pray with them, and they would draw strength from one another (see Mark 6:31).

His followers served at various times in both capacities, as replenishing relationships and as re-leech-ionships. The key, though, is that Christ knew when he needed to seek refuge in the arms of the Father, or those other select few, who recharged him for continued ministry.

When I think about someone who understood the difference between relationships and re-leech-ionships, I think about Daniel. He was a single man, articulate and handsome, who was deported from Jerusalem to Babylon during the Babylonian captivity of the Jews. Even during captivity in a foreign and pagan country, he was a man who was truly committed to God. While everyone else in his group was eating the fatty and unclean food from the king's table, he was eating only those things prescribed as clean according to the standards of the Mosaic Law.

Even though he was far away from his homeland in Babylon, he followed the rules God had laid down for the Hebrews and decided not to eat forbidden food. He stuck with water and vegetables. Daniel was also a strong man of prayer, and he went each day to the rooftop of the house in which he lived and prayed to God. There were many temptations in Babylon, many ways for him to stray, but he stayed committed to God.

The king loved Daniel, because he could see the kind of dedication and integrity he had. But some palace plotters got jealous of his status and played a cruel trick on him. They went to the king and played up to his ego, "Hey, King," they said, "You're pretty groovy. Why don't you set forth an edict stating that anyone who worships anything other than you will get thrown to the lions?" The king thought this sounded like a pretty good plan and set forth the edict just as they had proposed, but he had forgotten about the die-hard commitment of Daniel.

Then the jealous palace plotters said, "King, Daniel is on the rooftop praying to his God. He's worshiping something other than you." The king thought, *Oh, no, what have I done?* He had to throw Daniel, his main man, this committed man of God, into the lions' den. He was sure this would be the end of Daniel. There was no way a man could survive a night with Simba and his pals. He thought it was curtains for him. But the king did not know the real strength of Daniel's commitment and the miraculous power of his God.

The next morning Daniel emerged from the den unscathed, and the king declared his belief in Daniel's God, the one true God of Abraham, Isaac, and Jacob. The story, though, does not begin and end just with Daniel. Sure, Daniel was committed to God. He followed God's laws unwaveringly. He was a man of prayer, and he loved the Lord. But there is a reason Daniel was able to stay committed. He drew strength from the Lord, but he also had the godly encouragement and support of some rather bold and close-knit companions.

Think about it. Who did Daniel hang out with? Who were his best friends? Daniel surrounded himself with the three firemen of faith: Shadrach, Meshach, and Abednego. They understood Daniel's commitment level and supported him in that. These three men also practiced with Daniel the fundamentals of prayer and right living according to the law. Their friendship during this difficult time of captivity was a model of true relational commitment.

Don't discount the power of friendship in shaping your life as you grow in the Lord and serve him. With friends like Daniel had, you can find the strength and the courage to do many things that you would not be able to do alone. Yes, God does give us strength often to tread the waters of bold faith when no one else stands with us. But even the greatest men of faith in the Scriptures had strong companions who stood by them.

David and Jonathan, Paul and Timothy, Moses and Aaron, Joshua and Caleb, Jesus and his disciples—these are all examples of committed friends who stood by one another, replenished one another, and served God more effectively together. We need the encouragement and support of committed Christian friends. And we need to be willing to serve in that same capacity for others.

A Second Chance

You might be saying, "Well, Ed, this is interesting. I understand what you are saying about four-wheel driving, the Bimba principle, and re-leech-ionships. But Ed, you don't know me. I have messed up on so many commitments. I have broken promises to my spouse, my children, my friends, and my life has suffered. Is there a chance for me? Can I start afresh, start anew today?"

I can think of no better way to answer that question than by taking a page out of the life of Simon Peter, one of Jesus' most beloved disciples. On the night Jesus was betrayed, Simon Peter said these words to Jesus: "I will lay down my life for you." Then Jesus answered, "Will you really lay down your life for me? I tell you the truth, before the rooster crows, you will disown me three times!" (John 13:37–38). Peter said he was committed, and he truly believed he was committed, but Jesus knew the deep-seated fear in Peter's heart. When times would get tough, when Peter's world would begin to unravel upon the arrest of Jesus, and the doubts would creep in, Jesus knew the potential for weakness and disloyalty even before Peter did.

Jesus was arrested, taken to the house of Caiaphas, and thrown into a dungeon. Simon Peter trailed along to see what would happen and started warming himself by a fire outside. Three times people asked him if he knew Jesus, if he was associated with him. Peter was afraid they would arrest him too—he had the fear of commitment—so three times he denied his relationship with Jesus. He even started cursing.

Jesus was crucified and buried. Simon Peter, the man whose commitment had just cratered, went back to fishing. It was all he knew. Nothing seemed to make sense any more, so he returned to the one thing in his life that had always made sense: being a fisherman. And just like the first time, while fishing with his brother Andrew, he discovered again his true calling in life: being a fisher of men. Jesus came back to call him again, for the second time, to follow him. It was a call to recommitment.

Jesus rose from the dead and appeared on the shore of the Sea of Galilee. The sun was just coming up, that time of the morning when your eyes can play tricks on you. John 21 records an interchange between Jesus and these fishermen, but they did not recognize him at first. Jesus yelled out to them (I am paraphrasing), "Hey, guys, caught anything?" The fishermen replied, "No, we've fished all night, and nothing." Then Jesus said, "Throw your nets on the right side."

They did what he said, and there were so many fish they could barely pull the net up. The Bible records in John 21:11 that there were 153 fish. When Peter felt the size and weight of this catch, he just dove in and swam to shore. He knew something was up. Then he saw Jesus standing by a fire making breakfast. When Peter saw that fire, he must have thought about his dismal three-peat performance, how he had blown it, how he had cratered in commitment to his Lord.

What did Jesus do? What he does with all of us when we fail. Jesus reinstated him, forgave him, and empowered him. He called him back to commitment; he called him back to ministry with a simple question: "Do you love me?" Three times Jesus asked Peter this question: "The third time he said to him, 'Simon son of John, do you love me?' Peter was hurt because Jesus asked him the third time, 'Do you love me?' He said, 'Lord, you know all things; you know that I love you.' Jesus said, 'Feed my sheep'" (John 21:17).

Yes, it hurt a little to be asked the same question three times, but Christ asked it not for his own sake but for Peter's. Peter had denied him three times, and he needed to be reassured of his own commitment to Christ in the same manner as he had disowned him. Christ knew Peter loved him, but he wanted to be sure that Peter himself knew that he loved Christ. And the mark of his love was a commitment to love and care for Jesus' sheep, the people of God who would also be called to follow the Good Shepherd.

Simon Peter emerged from being reinstated by Christ as one of the most committed men ever to live. It doesn't matter what you have done or how many times you have blown it. There is no way we will ever blow it like Simon Peter did, and look what happened to him. There is another chance for you, another day for you. You can become a man or woman of great commitment because Christ is ultimately, irrevocably committed to you.

Despite humanity's dismal performance on the playing field of life, Jesus Christ demonstrated the ultimate act of commitment toward us: "While we were still sinners, Christ died for us" (Rom. 5:8). We were not worthy of it, but he paid the ultimate fine for your sins and mine. While Jesus was gasping for air, his lungs collapsing under his own weight, Satan was probably whispering in his ear, "Bail out. Throw in the towel. Don't stay in the game." But Jesus was committed and pledged himself to a position, no matter what the price: even death.

Very few things in life are worthy of our die-hard devotion—not even the Cowboys! In fact, only one is truly worthy. And no matter what you've done or how many times you've blown it, you still have a chance with Christ. He's committed himself completely to us. Now he's waiting for us to do the same—no reservations.

Facing Life's Phobias

TOO LEGIT TO QUIT

- Commit your way to the LORD, Trust also in Him, and He will do it (Ps. 37:5 NASB).
- "But your hearts must be fully committed to the LORD our God, to live by his decrees and obey his commands, as at this time" (1 Kings 8:61).

SHIFT INTO FOUR-WHEEL DRIVE

- Prepare for off-road situations by pledging yourself to a position no matter what.

THE BIMBA PRINCIPLE

- Do not be bound together with unbelievers; for what partnership have righteousness and lawlessness, or what fellowship has light with darkness? (2 Cor. 6:14 NASB).

RE-LEECH-IONSHIPS

- "Yet the news about him spread all the more, so that crowds of people came to hear him and to be healed of their sicknesses. But Jesus often withdrew to lonely places and prayed" (Luke 5:15–16).

A SECOND CHANCE

- Peter asked, "Lord, why can't I follow you now? I will lay down my life for you." Then Jesus answered, "Will you really lay down your life for me? I tell you the truth, before the rooster crows, you will disown me three times" (John 13:37–38).

- The third time he said to him, "Simon son of John, do you love me?" Peter was hurt because Jesus asked him the third time, "Do you love me?" He said, "Lord, you know all things; you know that I love you." Jesus said, "Feed my sheep" (John 21:17).

BREAKING THE GLASS BARRIER

Fear of Failure

In the life of every person alive today, certain things are brooding just beneath the surface. We keep them closely hidden, under wraps, buried deep inside of us. At certain times more than others, they show themselves. But often for only brief, fleeting moments. These things don't show themselves much because they are suppressed and held at bay by our own fears. Many people spend a lifetime ignoring these subsurface dwellers, confining them to the deep, dark recesses of their minds and hearts, never to be seen again.

What are these mysterious things lurking deep inside each one of us? They are our dreams of accomplishment and success. I am talking about those hopes, plans, and aspirations we have for our lives—the things we would tackle today if we knew we would succeed. I have never met anyone who does not have these kinds of dreams. Some people may keep them hidden more than others, but they are there. A rare few—and I can identify these people immediately—are fulfilling their dreams. They have taken risks in life that

chapter 4

few people are willing to take to achieve those deep-seated longings in their hearts.

If you are one of those rare people, you may not need to read this chapter. You have my permission just to skip it. But for the rest of us, I have a few simple questions. What's holding us back? What is keeping us from achieving those things that we know will make our lives more fulfilling? Why are we so hesitant to embark on those journeys, to try those things which will give us the deep satisfaction of accomplishment and success? What is holding our skill sets, our gifts, and our God-given talents at bay?

I believe the answer is fear. Specifically, we have paralyzed our hopes and dreams by our own fear of failure. We are afraid of trying something and messing up, making an attempt and falling flat on our faces. We are afraid of taking risks and of the hard work it would take to achieve success. Perhaps, for many of us, we are not as much afraid of failure as we are of success.

We have become so comfortable in our mediocre existence, not trying, not taking risks, and not stepping out, that we are not sure if we can really handle success—especially if it involves our deepest longings for achievement. So we opt for the security of the familiar rather than the risk of the unfamiliar. We might be thinking, "What if I fulfill those dreams and they are not all I expected them to be? What happens after I achieve that goal? What do I do next?"

The word *failure* sounds so defeating, so depressing. But we have several choices in the face of failure—and, I assure you, everyone fails at some time or another in life. Here are our choices when we fail: we can deny it, dwell on it, blame others for it, or we can allow it to mature and develop us. Only the last option gives us the strength and the courage to go on and to move toward achieving our goals.

One of the main reasons we all struggle with this fear of failure is that we have a skewed view of success. We don't understand what success is all about. As far as our culture is concerned, success is more or less relative. A successful basketball game for the Dallas Mavericks center may not be a successful game for the Los Angeles Lakers center. A successful meal prepared in one of our homes would not be seen as successful through the discriminating eyes of Martha Stewart. Who is more successful—the parent of an Olympic champion or the parent of a physically-challenged child?

The economy doesn't have to be booming for us to understand success. We don't have to see so-called "successful" people running around in great numbers, or driving around in their BMWs and Mercedess to be able to measure true success. Success from God's perspective is something completely different from success in the world's eyes. So before we start to deal with the fear of failure, I'm going to define true success as the Bible sets it forth. There are several underlying principles to this elusive state of being.

RELATIONAL OR CIRCUMSTANTIAL?

Close your eyes and think about the ultimate set of circumstances for your life. The ultimate appearance, the ultimate performance, the ultimate car and house and frequent-flyer plan— would those bring you lasting satisfaction? If all these circumstances fell into place, would your soul's thirst be quenched? I think that if you were at all honest with yourself, you would say no. It would be nice, but all of these materialistic perks wouldn't really cut it.

Israel was about to be given one of these materialistic perks. In light of that, God through Joshua, their leader, gave them some advice about where true success lies. The children of Israel, after wandering in the wilderness for forty years, were about to close the ultimate real estate deal and enter the Promised Land. Right before they did, this is what Joshua said: "Do not let this Book of the Law depart from your mouth; meditate on it day and night, so that you may be careful to do everything written in it. Then you will be prosperous and successful" (Josh. 1:8).

Do you see any extraneous circumstances here by which they were to measure success? Do you see anything about the weather, Wall Street, success against enemies? Any contingencies? No. This text just says to meditate on the Word of God day and night. Be careful to do everything written in it and then you will be prosperous and successful. This is a conditional statement, and the condition is obedience. You can still have all the materialistic trappings of what the world calls success; but without the favor of God, without the pleasure of being in his will, you do not have what the Bible calls success.

We read in Jeremiah 9:23–24 a similar admonition to follow the commands of the Lord in order to know true success: "This is what the LORD says: 'Let not the wise man boast of his wisdom or the strong man boast of his strength or the rich man boast of his riches, but let him who boasts boast about this: that he understands and knows me, that I am the LORD, who exercises kindness, justice and righteousness on earth, for in these I delight,' declares the LORD."

Understanding and knowing God: that is a relational thing, not a circumstantial thing. Our culture cries that success is about circumstances, the looks, the money, the power, and the prestige. It is not; it is about a personal relationship. It is about knowing God's Word, understanding it, and living it out. It is about having an interactive connection with him.

Do you know God through Christ? A lot of us fear this relationship. We say to ourselves, "I can't accept what God did for me through Christ. Jesus paid the price on the cross for all my shortcomings, all my failures, and rose again. I can't live up to that. If I accept him, I am going to fail him." We have the fear of failure even regarding the one relationship that will give us success.

Guess what? All followers of the Lord fail. We saw earlier how Peter failed the Lord miserably, on three separate occasions in one dismal night. Just like Peter, I will fail the Lord and so will you. But that is the beauty of the gospel of Christ: Jesus specializes in taking failures like you and me and reshaping us by his grace. Do you want to find success? Then you must understand, first of all, that success is built upon a relationship with God through Christ, not on the circumstances of wealth, position, talent, power, or anything else this earth has to offer.

CHARACTER OR ACHIEVEMENT?

All the biblical objectives concerning personal performance are character-driven. It doesn't matter whether you are a carpenter, commodities broker, coach, teacher, professor, or whatever. God says it doesn't matter: what matters is character. If you have godly character, if you reflect the nature and character of the Lord in all you do, then you will be successful no matter what your achievements are. Is that a great deal or what?

First Peter 1:6–7 is one of my favorite passages in the Bible dealing with character development. It focuses first on our failures, then moves to the glory that will be revealed through Christ's successes in our lives: "In this you greatly rejoice, though now for a little while you may have had to suffer grief in all kinds of trials. These have come so that your faith—of greater worth than gold, which perishes even though refined by fire—may be proved genuine and may result in praise, glory and honor when Jesus Christ is revealed."

Let's look at this text piece by piece. "Though now for a little while." A little while?—I talked to a man who told me, "Ed, I wish I could stay up 24-7. Then I could finally accomplish everything I want to do." He had it all wrong. None of us will ever accomplish everything we want. There just isn't enough time. But there is exactly enough time for us to accomplish everything God wants. All we have is a little while, but in God's economy, according to his measure of success, that is enough.

Take a look at the next piece: "You may have had to suffer grief in all kinds of trials." Does God sometimes cause us to fail, falter, and experience trials? Yes. We need trials, and we need failure, because we need discipline. The Bible says that God "disciplines those he loves" (Heb. 12:6). If I didn't discipline my four children, it would mean that I didn't really love them. God loves us enough to discipline us, as a father does in order to protect his children.

We also need trials for growth. God wants to grow us up and make us into better people. He will allow trials and temptations, difficulties and even failures in order to produce character in our lives.

The perennial example of this is Job. When I think of the trials and temptations Job faced, I realize that the hardships in my life are a joke in comparison. God allowed everything to be taken from Job—his possessions, his livelihood, and even his family. But the one thing that could not be taken away was his faith. The Evil One had the power to affect everything else in Job's life of a materialistic nature, but he could not touch his faith.

What happened? You know the story. Job persevered, and his character won the day. God knew the deep commitment of Job and that the testing of his faith would produce an even greater commitment. Job could have failed. He had the freedom of choice either to trust God or to curse him. He chose to trust him. God knows what we can take, and he tests us accordingly. The apostle Paul tells us that God will not allow us to be tempted or tried beyond what we are able to bear: "No temptation has seized you except what is common to man. And God is faithful; he will not let you be tempted beyond what you can bear. But when you are tempted, he will also provide a way out so that you can stand up under it" (1 Cor. 10:13).

If we fail, it's not because it was more than we could bear. We fail because we are not tapping into the resources God has given us for success: the Holy Spirit of God, the Word of God, and the power of prayer to God. Each time we stand up under the temptation, the trial, the hardship, the urge to quit, or the desire to bail out, our character becomes that much stronger for the next time we are tested.

God also gives us certain trials to prevent us from sinning, to keep us from messing up. If I tried to run my own life, I would mess up big-time. I would go through the wrong door, take the wrong path, and get off at the wrong exit. I'm thankful that God has shut this door in my face, blocked that path and that exit, even though at the time it looked like a trial. In reality, the obstacles he has placed in my path were there to protect me from doing something I should not be doing or going somewhere I should not be going. He has prevented me from sinning by using failures and trials in my life.

Continuing on in 1 Peter 1:6: "In all kinds of trials." This verse is saying that trials come in different makes and models. In the original language, "all kinds" means "various colors." We experience small trials and big trials, small failures and big failures. God uses it all, good and bad, to work together for good. We will be looking in greater depth at this passage later in the book, but I would be remiss if I did not quote Romans 8:28 at this point: "And we know that in all things God works for the good of those who love him, who have been called according to his purpose." What is the key here? This promise is for those who love God. It is for those who are called and who work out his plans and purposes in their lives.

So often we quote the beginning of this verse and conveniently leave off the last part. God wants good things for us, his children. He wants to use everything that happens in our lives, whether good or bad, whether joyful or hurtful, for our good and for his ultimate glory. But God's provision for us in this area is built upon a relationship of love, of mutual love—his for us and ours for him.

If you belong to God, if you have established that love relationship with him, he will allow the trials and temptations of life to be of benefit to you. Though you may not always understand how, he is working through all of these things to make us better people of faith.

The last part of the passage in 1 Peter 1:7 reads, "These have come so that your faith—of greater worth than gold, which perishes even though refined by fire—may be proved genuine and may result in praise, glory and honor." This is a little odd. Why does Simon Peter bring up gold? He's using the analogy of a goldsmith to say that God controls the temperature of the trials and failures.

A goldsmith goes through a long process to purify gold. He pours liquid gold into the smelting furnace and cranks up the temperature. As he heats it up, impurities rise to the surface and he scrapes them off. He turns up the heat again, more impurities rise, and he scrapes them off. He turns up the heat once more, more impurities rise, and he scrapes them off. He knows the gold is ready when he can see his reflection in it.

God has poured you and me into his smelting furnace. He turns up the heat with trials and failures, and all the impurities in our lives rise to the surface—anger, envy, and pride—where he can scrape them off. When he can see the reflection of his character in our lives, he knows we're ready to go. What kind of failures are you facing? What is fear doing to you? It's probably a gift from God, to cleanse you of impurities and make you ready for service.

I frequently talk about basketball because it was such a huge part of my life for so many years. From the time I was twelve years old to the age of nineteen, it was my goal to play major college basketball. I thought that if those circumstances fell into place, I would have achieved ultimate success.

I was fortunate enough to receive a scholarship to Florida State University, and during my sophomore year I broke into the starting lineup. I had several key opportunities to shine and do well. I was playing great in practice, but during the games I failed. I could not understand why this was happening. This was my dream. Why would God not allow me to play better in the games? Did he not want me to fulfill my dreams?

I believe that God shut the door on that dream in order to find a better dream. I believe that he allowed me to fail because if I had succeeded like I should have, I would be at least four years behind where I am today: spiritually, relationally, and emotionally. I would have stayed at Florida State and done the whole college athletics deal. Instead, God tapped me on the shoulder and said, "Ed, I want you to give up your full scholarship and go into the ministry."

I walked into my coach's office and said, "Coach Williams, I feel led to go into the ministry. I appreciate everything you and the university have done for me, but I want to give up the scholarship." That was very difficult for me because I had so identified with the game of basketball for so many years. It meant taking a huge risk. It meant giving up what I thought would bring me success and fulfillment and trusting God to give me satisfaction in life.

Yes, in a sense I had failed at my dream. But through that failure, God taught me something: success is not scoring twenty points a game or being on the all-conference team. I learned through that experience that God uses failure for greater purposes. I also began to understand the nature of true success.

Success from God's perspective is character driven. I learned that, even though I shot many air balls, even though I messed up many times, I was successful because I was living my life as a Christian witness. I realized that God allowed that failure to happen to get me out of one situation and put me somewhere else. At the time, I didn't get it. But I managed to say, "God, I trust you."

What failure are you going through? What trial are you going through? Are you denying it, dwelling on it, and blaming others for it? Or are you saying, "God, I don't get it now, but I want you to use this time to develop me." It's all about character.

God wants to see courage, commitment, discipline, and vision. He doesn't care how many zeroes appear on the paycheck or how many toys and trinkets we collect. He doesn't care where we live or what we drive. Godly character drives true success.

MANAGEMENT OR OWNERSHIP?

Success in the world is measured by how much we own, how much we accumulate, and how many toys we collect. But in the eyes of God, we don't own one thing. We came into this life with nothing, and we'll leave this life with nothing.

"Well, Ed, you don't understand, man. I pulled myself up by the bootstraps. You don't realize what I have made of my life, coming from the background I have." How did you get to where you are? Who gave you the creativity, the drive, the people skills to get there? Who blessed you, enabled you, and empowered you? God gave it to you with the snap of a finger, and he can take it away just as quickly.

Jesus illustrated this idea beautifully with the parable of the talents in Matthew 25. In the time of Jesus, the talent was the largest unit of silver and equivalent to the value of an ox.[1] Jesus told his disciples a story about a wealthy landowner who was going out of town on a business trip. Before leaving, he gave one of his servants five talents, another two talents, and a third one talent, with the hopes that they would invest the money for him while he was away.

During the landowner's absence, here is what happened. The servant with five talents invested in tech stocks, or something like that, and doubled his money. The one who had two talents parleyed his into four talents. And the one with one talent dug a hole and sat on it.

The wealthy landowner came back in town and checked the accounts. He said to the first two servants, "Good for you. You were faithful with a little; now I'll entrust you with a lot." But to the servant who had sat on his talent he said, in effect, "Get out of my face," and divided the talent among the others.

What is the point of this story? Was the landowner being unfair? Jesus is saying that we are to develop our gifts and abilities. I am to invest my gifts, abilities, and talents and to use them and invest them as an act of worship to God. I am not supposed to take my abilities and sit on them. I should use them within the context of marriage, within the context of the local church, and within the context of a career for the glory of God, to advance his kingdom.

As I develop this gift and give it back to God, God will say, "Well done. I've given you the ability to communicate, to make money, to organize, to be creative. You have developed those abilities, and that's an act of worship."

There is more wealth today than ever before in our nation. But a lot of us are selfish and greedy. As our earnings go up, our yearnings go up, and we just throw pocket change at God and the church. One day he will come back and look at us, and a lot of people who call themselves Christ-followers will hang their heads in shame: their greed and selfishness kept them from God's will. We really don't have any stuff. Our stuff is all God's. It is not about giving back to God. It is about investing what is already his to begin with.

A pilot sits in the cockpit of his plane and punches buttons to test his machinery. He can tell that the plane is functioning and it's ready to go. God has a quick test-button that he can push in your life called the *resource button.*

God talks a lot about money because he knows we all deal with greed and think our possessions belong to us. When God pushes that button, what do you do? Do you live by a budget: give him 10 percent, and save 10 percent? Success is about managing what our Lord has given us to manage, not owning possessions we think we've earned. And that includes the talents and skills he has given us. We did not earn those or deserve those. God gave us all that we have and all that we are to bring glory to him, to serve him, and to minister to others. That is stewardship.

Now that we have a better understanding of biblical success, let's take a look at some examples of how people in the Bible have dealt with the fear of failure.

BEHIND THE BAGGAGE OR IN THE LIGHT?

Once there was a guy named Saul. Saul was gifted, articulate, handsome, and tall—head and shoulders above other people. The Israelites started acting like kids: "God, the neighboring nations have a king. How come we don't get a king? We want a king!" Parents today may recognize similar tantrums: "Mom, Johnny has that video game, why can't I get it?" or "Dad, they get to stay out until midnight; it's not fair!"

God said, "You don't know what you're asking for, but OK. I'll give you a king." Samuel, God's prophet, tapped Saul on the shoulder for the job. Saul's peers, the guys he had gone to Palestine High with, started making fun of Saul. They said things like, "What, Saul as a king? What a joke!" (see 1 Sam. 10:11).

Saul tuned into those conversations and thought, *Maybe I am a joke. Maybe I'd be a terrible king.* He fell into the trap that many of us fall into by listening to others before listening to God. The approval of his peers meant more to Saul than the calling of God on his life.

Samuel set up a big press conference at Mizpah to announce Saul to the entire nation of Israel. It was time for Saul to go public. But when the big moment arrived, they couldn't find him. He was hiding behind the baggage, consumed with the fear of failure. He had let the opinion of his peers feed his fears, and Saul literally tried to hide from his responsibility before God and the people of Israel.

Do you do that? Are others' words keeping you from a great plan, dream, or aspiration? Are you hiding behind baggage? Has God impressed something upon your heart that he wants you to do? Are you being pulled in a certain direction by the gentle leading of the Holy Spirit? But instead of listening to God and drawing strength from him, are you tuning in to the negativity of others?

Think of Noah by way of contrast to Saul. Noah was building a huge boat on dry land at a time when no one had ever even seen rain before. People were probably laughing at him, making fun of him. Can you imagine the ridicule he must have faced? But he didn't do what Saul did—he didn't hide behind a stack of lumber or drive the forklift into the back forty. He just kept building. Sure, Noah was fearful; he was human. But he faced his fears. And because he heard the voice of God rather than the negative talk, he went to higher ground while the naysayers and the trash-talkers drowned.

You have a choice to make about whose words and opinions are going to be more important in your estimation. Will you be like Saul, so fearful of what others think that you literally hide yourself from the responsibilities and opportunities that await you? Or will you be like Noah? Will you listen to God and trust him to give you the strength to persevere even in the midst of negative pressure from others?

WEAKNESSES OR STRENGTHS?

If we are to understand failure, we also have to come to grips with our strengths and weaknesses. Even Moses, the great patriarch of the Jewish faith, the receiver of the law, the deliverer of the children of Israel out of the hands of Pharaoh, had weaknesses. And he stood before God one day, trembling in fear as a bush burned in front of him but was not consumed, reciting the weaknesses he perceived would keep him from success.

God said, "Moses, I want you to deliver the children of Israel out of Egypt. I want you to talk to them and share my vision with them."

Moses said, "No way, God. I stutter and stumble. I can't speak in front of people." Moses was looking at his weaknesses, his shortcomings, and his failures. He was frozen with anxiety and fear.

Is God telling you to do something, only to hear a similar response by you? Are you giving in to your weaknesses and thinking to yourself, "Oh, no, God can't use a failure like me." God heard and understood Moses' fears. He knew what Moses' weaknesses were. The issue, though, was not Moses' weakness; it was God's power. And he gave Moses a staff as a proof of his power to both Pharaoh and the people of Israel.

Think also of David, the shepherd boy turned king. David fought Goliath when he was just a teenager, while he was still going through puberty. While still listening to the Back Street Boys, with pimples all over his face, having never fought another human being, he took on Goliath: a 9-foot, 550-pound giant with a major chip on his shoulder against the Israelites. What was David's secret to success? He played to God's strengths, not his own. He said, "I have taken out the lion. I have taken out the bear. I can do it. God is on my side, and he will give me victory." God provided the resources—the stones and the sling—and David took the giant out.

Are you giving in to your weaknesses, focusing on them instead of on God's power? God can use you in spite of your shortcomings? Consider 2 Corinthians 12:9–10, "But he said to me, 'My grace is sufficient for you, for my power is made perfect in weakness.' Therefore I will boast all the more gladly about my weaknesses, so that Christ's power may rest on me. That is why, for Christ's sake, I delight in weaknesses, in insults, in hardships, in persecutions, in difficulties. For when I am weak, then I am strong." Is that your attitude toward weakness? Are you focusing on yourself and your inabilities or on God and his abilities?

One of the great paradoxes of the Christian life is that God's power is made known and realized through the weaknesses of his people. If you want to break through to success, you have to focus not on your strengths but on God's strength being made perfect in your shortcomings. Then, and only then, does God truly receive the glory for everything you do, because others can clearly see that your accomplishments are made possible by God's power, not yours.

EXAGGERATE OR ENGAGE?

The Hebrews were standing at the edge of the Promised Land for the first time, and God told them to send out twelve spies to check the land. Ten of the twelve came back and said, "Oh, no, we can't do it! There are giants in the land. The sons of Anak are there." Believe it or not, the sons of Anak were distant relatives of Goliath. "We can't do it. The cities are fortified. The walls are thirty feet thick." They were exaggerating the obstacles to justify their fears and unwillingness to do what needed to be done.

How did the other two spies respond? Basically, they came back and said, "God has promised us this land, and we can overcome." Their focus was not on exaggerating all of the problems and obstacles in their path but on engaging in the task to which God had called them.

Maybe you'll recognize more readily some of these modern-day excuses. "I can't start this business—I don't have the capital, and all of these government requirements are too hard for me to understand." Or how about this: "I'll never be able to make sense of my blended family—the kids fight all the time, and these joint custody arrangements are never going to work out." Or maybe this is more familiar: "If I told the truth to my boss about what happened, I'd be fired. It's not worth the risk to be honest." We still love to exaggerate the obstacles in our lives today. Because we fear an uncertain outcome and don't trust God for success, we exaggerate and rationalize rather than engage.

Sometimes God will intentionally allow us to feel outgunned, outmanned, and outmaneuvered so that we will know that it was God who won the battle. Look at the battle that Gideon faced in Judges 7. Gideon had thirty-two thousand soldiers ready to fight, but God told him to cut the army down to three hundred. This probably didn't make any more sense to Gideon than it does to us. Why would God ask Gideon to do such a seemingly foolish thing? It's not surprising that, in light of this unorthodox battle strategy, Gideon was fearful about the outcome of this battle.

The incredible thing about this story is not Gideon's fear but God's patient response. Sensing Gideon's fear, God actually invited Gideon to sneak into enemy territory and overhear a conversation that would reassure him about the victory to come. It turned out that God had been communicating through dreams to Israel's enemies, the Midianites, that Gideon would overtake them. And Gideon was able to listen as one of the Midianite soldiers recalled his dream to a fellow soldier about Israel's army rolling over them.

The enemies of God and Israel had reason to fear failure, especially when they had been given specific visions of their impending doom. There is an appropriate fear for those outside of the safety, protection, and will of the Almighty. At the same time God gives a sense of calm assurance of ultimate victory, even despite occasional setbacks, for those who are obedient, for those who are on the Lord's side. Gideon took out the army and won the battle. He was fearful, but he stopped exaggerating the obstacles, looking at them in light of God's strength, not his own, and engaged the enemy.

At the end of the day, success has everything to do with God and very little to do with you. If you're yielded to his agenda, his timing, and his strength, failure is not an option—because God is not a failure.

Facing Life's Phobias

RELATIONAL OR CIRCUMSTANTIAL?

- "Do not let this Book of the Law depart from your mouth; meditate on it day and night, so that you may be careful to do everything written in it. Then you will be prosperous and successful" (Josh. 1:8).

- This is what the LORD says: "Let not the wise man boast of his wisdom or the strong man boast of his strength or the rich man boast of his riches, but let him who boasts boast about this: that he understands and knows me, that I am the LORD, who exercises kindness, justice and righteousness on earth, for in these I delight," declares the LORD (Jer. 9:23–24).

CHARACTER OR ACHIEVEMENT?

- In this you greatly rejoice, though now for a little while you may have had to suffer grief in all kinds of trials. These have come so that your faith—of greater worth than gold, which perishes even though refined by fire—may be proved genuine and may result in praise, glory and honor when Jesus Christ is revealed (1 Pet. 1:6–7).

- No temptation has seized you except what is common to man. And God is faithful; he will not let you be tempted beyond what you can bear. But when you are tempted, he will also provide a way out so that you can stand up under it (1 Cor. 10:13).

- And we know that in all things God works for the good of those who love him, who have been called according to his purpose (Rom. 8:28).

MANAGEMENT OR OWNERSHIP?

- "His master replied, 'Well done, good and faithful servant! You have been faithful with a few things; I will put you in charge of many things. Come and share your master's happiness!'" (Matt. 25:21).

BEHIND THE BAGGAGE OR IN THE LIGHT?

- Finally Saul son of Kish was chosen. But when they looked for him, he was not to be found. So they inquired further of the LORD, "Has the man come here yet?" And the LORD said, "Yes, he has hidden himself among the baggage" (1 Sam. 10:21b–22).

- "Noah did everything just as God commanded him" (Gen. 6:22).

WEAKNESSES OR STRENGTHS?

- But he said to me, "My grace is sufficient for you, for my power is made perfect in weakness. Therefore I will boast all the more gladly about my weaknesses, so that Christ's power may rest on me. That is why, for Christ's sake, I delight in weaknesses, in insults, in hardships, in persecutions, in difficulties. For when I am weak, then I am strong" (2 Cor. 12:9–10).

EXAGGERATE OR ENGAGE?

- They gave Moses this account: "We went into the land to which you sent us, and it does flow with milk and honey! Here is its fruit. But the people who live there are powerful, and the cities are fortified and very large" (Num. 13:27–28a).
- Then Caleb silenced the people before Moses and said, "We should go up and take possession of the land, for we can certainly do it" (Num. 13:30).
- During that night the LORD said to Gideon, "Get up, go down against the camp, because I am going to give it into your hands. If you are afraid to attack, go down to the camp with your servant Purah and listen to what they are saying. Afterward, you will be encouraged to attack the camp" (Judg. 7:9–11).
- When Gideon heard the dream and its interpretation, he worshiped God. He returned to the camp of Israel and called out, "Get up! The LORD has given the Midianite camp into your hands" (Judg. 7:15).

TABLE FOR ONE

Fear of Loneliness

Swiss psychiatrist Paul Toarnier called it the most devastating malady of this age. Billy Graham has commented that it is man's greatest problem. Mother Teresa once said that it is easier to fill a hungry stomach than to fill an empty heart. Thomas Wolfe said that it is the central and inevitable fact of human existence.

Ask the divorcee who has just moved into the one-bedroom apartment. Talk to the parent whose arms still ache because of their deceased child. Speak with the single man or woman who has just ended the engagement. Observe the family who has just been transferred in from another city. Ask them to tell you about their loneliness.

Loneliness is not a natural thing, and we try to steer clear of it at every turn. But even in the midst of people, and sometimes especially there, our loneliness is magnified. When we find ourselves in a crowded restaurant or a crowded church, looking at people connecting and interacting, we feel relationally ripped off, like the have-nots looking at the haves.

chapter 5

I know it is hard to believe, but many people in our ever-growing society are dealing with large amounts of loneliness. You may be one of those people. You know how to mask it. You know how to keep it at arms length. You know how to explain it away, but the cold reality is that you feel and experience loneliness on a regular basis.

Loneliness can be defined as being without companionship. It is not the same as being alone. Being alone is different from loneliness. Scripture commands us to take time to be alone, alone with our thoughts, alone with our prayers, in solitude and silence. Sometimes, though, we are afraid to be alone, because we know if we are by ourselves we will have to deal with our loneliness. Well, if we are to understand and conquer this fear, we need to take a hard look within and without at our attempts to cover up loneliness, as well as the precipitating factors that drive this common human condition.

I want to address, first of all, the things we do to mask feelings of loneliness and the things that keep us from honestly confronting them. We live in a time of constant commotion and activity. The noise of our lives serves as a kind of security blanket against the realization of our need for relational connection. The need always to have cell phones ringing and beepers buzzing and fax machines whining and computers E-mailing has helped to cover over a deeper need, whether felt or unfelt.

Our tethered connection to technology often keeps us from relating to others, because we no longer have to relate to real human beings to accomplish the tasks of day-to-day living. Little do we realize, though, as we go about our technologically driven existence, that we are encouraging by our behavior the very thing we most fear: a life of isolation that is devoid of meaningful human contact.

Technology is not the only culprit. Our attitude toward people often isolates us from them. Our culture is so into doing deals, holding conferences, and having meetings that we have become a people of clients rather than a people of relationships. We no longer really understand what it means to live in true intimacy and community with others. In short, we are a lonely people, and we have no one to blame but ourselves.

The Bible relates to us over and over again, from the very beginning in the Garden of Eden, that it is not good for us to be alone. It would be easy to say, "God does not want you to be alone, so stop fearing loneliness." You can close the book, "The End." But we can't do that. It is not that simple. The Bible not only cautions us against isolation, but it also shows us how to break down the walls and masks that isolate us and how to break through to connectedness on several different levels.

In this chapter, I want to identify three levels of loneliness and then show you how to connect on the relational levels they represent. You may be saying to yourself, "Me, lonely. Are you kidding—me?" I will guarantee you something. Everyone, including me, deals with one or more of these levels of loneliness.

Understanding and overcoming loneliness is critical to living the abundant Christian life. Larry Crabb says it well in his insightful book, *Understanding Who You Are:* "Life in Christ is all about relationships, with God, others, and ourselves. When we reduce Christianity to a series of steps for handling life better or a set of truths to believe or a list of things to do, we miss the whole point of the gospel."[1] It's all about relationships. Loneliness is the symptom of some unmet relational need. First of all, though, we must understand that we will never find ultimate relational fulfillment, in any relationship, until the relational need with God is met.

SPIRITUAL LONGINGS

God created us so he could have fellowship with us. The Bible was written that we might know God. Christ came into the world so we could be reconciled to God. Sadly, though, many people live their lives outside of a relationship with God, and they are spiritually lonely. This represents the first and most significant level of loneliness: *spiritual loneliness.*

The Bible says that we are all born lonely, separated from God. The prophet Isaiah referred to this: "But your iniquities have separated you from your God; your sins have hidden his face from you, so that he will not hear" (Isa. 59:2). When God saw our separation, when he saw the implications of our state of spiritual loneliness, he didn't just say, "Well, too bad for you. I guess you will have to live a lonely life." God did something: he took the initiative to break the cycle of loneliness.

You may have a gnawing sense that something is not right in your life. You have been on a search for significance. You thought that joining a certain club or playing on the right team or climbing the corporate ladder would do it, but nothing has brought the meaning for which you have been searching.

You thought making a certain amount of money would do it, but the money has lost its luster. You thought that getting married to that certain person would do it, but that, too, has left you empty. You thought that having a couple of children to carry on your legacy would do it, but they have not filled the hole in your heart.

You know down deep that you are still lonely. You are spiritually lonely. I don't care what you do, how much money you can pile up, how many toys and things you can accumulate; it will not fill that void in your life. The math does not work. Maybe you need to deal with this first level of loneliness in the most basic and fundamental sense. Maybe you need to allow Jesus Christ to come into your life so you can be reconciled with God.

We serve an initiative-taking God. When God saw our loneliness, this chasm, this gap caused by our sinfulness, he sent Christ to live a perfect life and to die on the cross for our sins and rise again. That is the message of Christianity. When Jesus was dying on the cross, what did he say? Some of his last words were chilling: "My God, my God, why have you forsaken me?" (Matt. 27:46b). Why have you, God, turned your back on me? Why this loneliness, God?

When Jesus was hanging on the cross, God the Father had to turn his back on his Son. He had to separate himself from his Son. Jesus felt this spiritual level of loneliness, to a point that we cannot even express in words, as he paid for our sins. He did not want us to go through life and eternity missing true community with God. He paved the way for us to have a personal relationship with God the Father.

It is our loneliness that drives us to our knees. It is our loneliness that motivates us to become Christ-followers. Talk to people who have just stepped over the line. Talk to people who have been followers of the Lord for years and years. They will tell you that they felt lonely—a gnawing sense that something was wrong. They had a hole in their hearts that brought them to a place of receiving Christ.

Maybe you are there, with that same gnawing feeling at the core of your being. You can satisfy your spiritual longings only by establishing a personal relationship with God, and it all begins by placing your faith and trust in Jesus Christ.

What if you are a believer? What if you have stepped over the line? What if you are like me and you know Christ personally, but now and then you still feel a sense of loneliness? We know, if we have accepted Christ, that we can never experience true loneliness again. But we can still have feelings of loneliness from time to time. What do we do with those feelings when loneliness rears its ugly head and tries to knock us down?

We have to deal with the feelings. And the feelings are subject to our decision-making capacity fueled by the Holy Spirit of God. We can either take those feelings of loneliness and allow them to push us away from God, or we can allow those feelings to push us toward God. We can pray, "God, I am feeling feelings of loneliness. I know I am not truly lonely because I know you. But I am still feeling the feelings. God, fill the gap in my life. Help me, God, with your grace, love, and power, to experience you in a deeper way to satisfy these level-one longings in my heart."

The apostle Paul experienced loneliness. In 2 Timothy 4:16, he declared, "At my first defense, no one came to my support, but everyone deserted me." Have you ever felt that you are the only person standing for Christ at the office? Do feel like you are the only real Christian around the neighborhood? Or perhaps you may even be standing alone for Christ in your family. You are the only one in your family who has made a faith commitment, and sometimes the feelings of loneliness are unbearable. Paul continues in verse 17, "But the Lord stood at my side and gave me strength." We must recognize our need for and draw strength from the companionship of Christ.

What did Jesus say to his disciples right before he left this earth and went to heaven? "And surely I am with you always, to the very end of the age" (Matt. 28:20b). Do you have that level-one loneliness quenched? Have you met God through Christ? Or if you know him, are you allowing the feelings of loneliness that sometimes assault you to push you closer and deeper in your relationship with him? Christ has always been there; he is waiting for you to make the move toward him.

RELATIONAL LONGINGS

I call the next level of loneliness level-two or relational loneliness. If you go back to the first book of the Bible, Genesis, and read over the first two or three chapters, you will see God creating. After every creative act, God stepped back and said, "It is good." Then God made man in his image, and God said, "It is very good." Suddenly, though, in Genesis 2:18, something changes. Adam, the first man, was fulfilled in his level-one connectedness; he was connected with God. He was interacting with him in a way that we will not experience until we get to heaven.

But God saw a level-two problem, and he labeled something as "not good" for the first time, "The LORD God said, 'It is not good for the man to be alone. I will make a helper suitable for him'" (Gen. 2:18).

119

God did not deny the need that Adam had for human companionship. God did not try to explain it away. He said there was a level two need and that he would make someone suitable for Adam. God took the initiative with Adam, and he took the initiative again with Christ. We serve a God who steps out of the shadows and is proactive. God's game plan is basic. He wants us to have a vibrant connection with him through Christ, and he also wants us to walk deeply in relationships with others. That is God's agenda for our lives.

Jesus summarized the importance of these two relational levels in a couple of succinct sentences in Matthew 22:37–39. In response to a question about which was the greatest commandment, he said: "'Love the Lord your God (this indicates intention) with all your heart and with all your soul and with all your mind (this indicates the level of intensity).' This is the first (level one) and greatest commandment. And the second (level two) is like it: 'Love (intention) your neighbor as yourself (intensity)'" (parenthetical comments added).

So we have intentionality, a decision to love, followed by intensity. Level one, an intentional decision to love God with all of your being, comes first. And level two, an intentional decision to love others as you love yourself, comes second.

The Bible never tells us to love ourselves. That is a given. I love myself. You love yourself too. But when I am asked to love my neighbor as myself, that is a tall order. You might say, "I want to have deep relationships. I really want to connect with others." Many of us say that, but in reality we don't mean it.

The truth of the matter is that most people, including Christians, have hydroplane relationships. Hydroplaning is when you are driving and you hit a patch of water or ice, and the wheels are not really on the pavement. They are just skimming the surface of the ice. We are just sliding around on the surface and not making contact with the road. We do the same thing in relationships.

We may have known people for a long time, but we are still talking about the same stuff: the weather, sports, and current events. We are fearful to relate to them on a deep level. Why? We say to ourselves, "If they really perused the portfolio of my problems, they would reject me. They wouldn't like me. They would not believe what I am dealing with or what I have done or what I am struggling with. They would just keep me at arm's length."

That is not true. If we were to come clean and commit both our level-one and level-two loneliness to God, and really began to share who we are with people, people would sigh and tell us that they are struggling with the same things, dealing with the same issues. The key is to keep both of these levels in balance. Do not put level-one expectations on level-two relationships. Have you ever done that before? Sometimes we put too much weight, too much of a burden, on the shoulders of human beings.

We have an elevator in our church complex. There is a sign in it saying the maximum capacity is twenty-five hundred pounds. If the maximum capacity is exceeded, whoever is on that elevator will be in trouble. During our Christmas Eve service, the elevator stalled between floors because there was too much weight on it.

If we turn to human relationships to satisfy our relational loneliness before turning to God to satisfy our spiritual loneliness, we are in for trouble. We cannot dump all of our relational and spiritual stuff, with all the expectations and pressures, on human relationships.

There is a maximum capacity sign on every human relationship. And although the sign says maximum capacity twenty-five hundred pounds, we are putting thousands of pounds on humans and expecting them to meet needs that only God can meet. No wonder we have burned through so many relationships. No wonder we have gone through so many marriages.

You cannot expect your spouse to meet needs that only God can meet. You can't put those kinds of expectations on your wife or your husband or your friend. My friends can't deliver me from evil. My friends cannot answer my prayers. My friends cannot forgive me of my sins or guide me or lead me. Only God can do that.

We sometimes become so intensive, so clingy, and so whiney in human relationships that we forget about level-one needs. We put so much pressure on the other person that we totally turn them off to wanting to relate to us at all. They begin to say, "Man, I need some space. You are smothering me." They push us away, and we feel rejected.

If that is happening to you, don't despair. Go back to level one and start over. Your Savior must be the source of your relational strength. When you connect with him, when you walk with him, when you talk with him, then you have some real power to bring to human relationships. A true friend is going to point you to Christ. A true friend will deepen your relationship with him. A true friend sees himself as an extension of God in the relationship. And you can find those types of friends as you become that kind of friend to others.

God is a jealous God—I am going to talk about that in the next chapter—and, if you are putting superhuman expectations on a relationship, God will find a way to end the relationship. God must be first in your life because he knows it is the only way you will find true fulfillment at any level.

Are you serious about level two? Do you really want those deep-water relationships? Let me give several suggestions to help make this happen on a practical level.

First, take regular relational risks. Every time we take a relational risk, we are reflecting the character and nature of God. When we do not take those risks, when we hide behind our fears, we are disobeying God. Proverbs 18:24 says, "A man who has friends must himself be friendly" (NKJV). We all want friends. And if you want to have friends, you need to ask yourself a couple of questions. What kind of friend would I like to have? Am I willing to be that kind of friend?

I have moved around many times in my life. I have moved from Canton, North Carolina, to Taylor, South Carolina, to Columbia, South Carolina, to Houston, Texas, to Tallahassee, Florida, back to Houston, Texas, and from there to Dallas, Texas. A while back I was looking at the relationships God has given me over the years and asking myself what the common thread was in those relationships. What quality or qualities made those relationships work? Then it came to me. I have taken the initiative in almost every relationship I have had. I have taken regular relational risks. I knew that if I was going to have deep friendships, I had to show myself friendly. More than that, I had to be vulnerable with those with whom I wanted to develop deeper relationships.

Here is what many of us do in the church in regard to relationships. Week in and week out we walk into the church, and we look for a seat. We think to ourselves, *Boy, there sure are a lot of people here. This is a big church.* We find our seat, and we just sit there. And then, after a while, maybe several months, we say to ourselves, "No one talked to me. No one came up to me. This church is just not a friendly place. It is full of snobs."

Then we go to another church and do the same thing again. After a while we say, "No one talked to me. No one came up to me. I guess that church is just full of snobs too. No one cares about me. I want to relate to people. I want to talk to people, but no one comes up to me."

God does not want to hear those weak excuses. He wants you to take relational risks. A person who wants friends must show himself to be a friendly person. It's time to step out and see what God has in store for you. There is no telling what God will do through an ordinary person like you who is willing to take an ordinary relational risk. Gallup says that the average church member knows 67 people per church, whether the church has 150, 11,000, or 25,000 people.

I pastor a large church, and I think large churches are great. But if you are in a smaller church, you have the same relational potential available. One great thing about a larger church, though, is that your base for potential relationships is much larger. If you meet somebody and you don't connect, there are many other opportunities out there to establish meaningful relationships. Wherever you have chosen as your church home, however, the choice is up to you, the initiative must be yours, to begin to develop the kind of relationships that will fill your level-two longings.

I would hate to get to the end of my life and have God say, "Ed, you know you did a pretty good job at doing this and doing that. However, I had so many relational opportunities for you at the church. And Ed, you just sat there and waited for people to come up to you. You just sat there and didn't take initiative. I wanted this person to help you. I was going to speak through this person in your life, but you missed out."

The church is to be a social place. I am not just making this up. Read about the early church in Acts 2. They met together in the temple courts, and then they met from house to house. They were highly social and highly relational in every aspect of what they did as a church body. If we are going to reach the level of community exhibited by the early church, we must take the relational risks necessary to bring people into the inner spheres of our lives.

Here is another suggestion, and I am still talking about level-two relational needs. This suggestion is one you rarely hear articulated in a church, but it is articulated in Scripture and even commanded of Christians. The Bible tells us that we are to show hospitality to others, especially to our brothers and sisters in the Lord: "Offer hospitality to one another without grumbling" (1 Pet. 4:9).

I am talking about that initiative-taking, hand-shaking, house-warming, guest-comforting mentality that says, "Come on out with us for a hamburger" or "Pour some more water in the soup. Let's have a good time." That is hospitality. Is your life marked with a spirit of hospitality?

The Lord hit me with a bolo punch a few years ago regarding what hospitality really is. I was on a mission trip in Korea with Lisa, my wife. A missionary invited us over to her two-room house to spend the night. She served us Spam and crackers with Kool-Aid. She threw a mat on the floor for us to sleep on. She did not say, "Well, I'm sorry. This is all I can serve. This is all I have."

This generous woman was hospitable with what God had given her. Hospitality is sharing what you have with others for the glory of God. Yet a lot of us here in America live in three-, four-, five-, or six-bedroom homes and have not invited anyone over yet.

We throw out these lame excuses for not opening up our homes: "It would take me too long to clean the house and get it ready." "I want to furnish and decorate the house just right before I have people over to see it." "I can't really cook that well." "I don't know what to say to my guests."

Don't let your relational fears or your pride keep you from sharing your home with others. It is time to step out, take a relational risk, and open up your home just the way it is. You will find that if you just make some small attempts at hospitality, you will enjoy it and wish you had started doing it much earlier.

Let me interject here what the purpose of hospitality is. It is not to impress our friends or to raise our social status up a notch in our church or neighborhood. Hospitality is about community, about providing an outlet where real relationships can grow. It is about honoring your guests and valuing them as people.

You may remember the story of Jesus going to the home of Martha and her sister Mary for a meal. Martha was busying herself with all the cooking, the preparations, the cleaning and so on. She wanted to impress her Lord. She wanted to be noticed for all she was doing, and she complained to Jesus that Mary was not doing any of the work but was getting all the attention.

Mary was sitting at the feet of Jesus talking and listening to him. She wanted to know Jesus. She did not want to be noticed as much as she wanted to notice, observe, and learn from all Jesus had to offer. Her purpose was to get to know him and value him as their guest.

For Mary and for Jesus, a simple meal and good conversation were all that was required. But Martha went overboard and in all her busyness forgot why Jesus was there in the first place. I love Jesus' reply to Martha, in response to her complaint, because it cuts to the core of Martha's problem, "'Martha, Martha,' the Lord answered, 'you are worried and upset about many things, but only one thing is needed. Mary has chosen what is better, and it will not be taken away from her'" (Luke 10:41–42).

Remember the why of hospitality. Don't be worried and upset about all the things you think you need to do to entertain your guests. The Lord of lords required only a simple meal and fellowship with his hosts. The same simplicity is all he asks of you as you open up your home to others.

If you are not opening up your home to others on a regular basis, you are missing some great blessings from God himself. The writer of Hebrews said, "Do not forget to entertain strangers, for by so doing some people have entertained angels without knowing it" (Heb. 13:2). I can't promise anything, but by practicing hospitality to friends and strangers alike, you never know whom God might send your way.

Taking it a step deeper, the entire church should be built on hospitality. If you are involved in a local church, you are only one step away from level-two community by getting involved in a small-group ministry at your church. I cannot describe to you the letters we receive at Fellowship Church week in and week out about the blessings of small groups. Yes, we are commanded to worship God corporately, but true life-change takes place in small-group settings. One of the things we say often at Fellowship is that we want to grow smaller while we grow larger.

Again, don't let fear dictate your actions in this regard. It is easy to make excuses for not getting involved in a small group. "Well, Ed, they might ask me a question about the Bible, and I don't know that much about the Bible. They might put me on the spot." I am not talking about attending a seminary class. A small group is a place where sharing, caring, and praying take place. It is a place where you can learn about God's Word *together* and find ways to apply it to your lives *together*. You are not going to be tested or prodded or poked. At least, if it is a biblically functioning group within a biblically functioning church, you should not be.

I must also emphasize the importance of connecting with a group like this before the crises in life hit you. If you do not have a small-group ministry in your church, then find a way to start one. Or find a church that has one. We have to connect in this way in order to build community. We have to connect intimately with people in order to deal with the loneliness we all feel. We have to connect because of the value each of us brings to the small-group table.

If you are lonely, for the most part, you are lazy. If you are lonely, you need to get outside of yourself. I can't take you and grab you by the dress or the shirt and drag you into a small-group situation. You must make the choice. You must make the effort to get involved.

It saddens me that so many people have gone to church year after year without connecting in this way. One day when the bottom drops out, who will help you? Who will serve you? Who will support you? Who will take care of you? Who will be your real friends?

What are the fringe benefits of going deeper relationally? Let me hit a couple of them briefly. I am still talking about level-two or human relationships. First of all, it will mature you like nothing else will. When you think about spiritual maturity, when you study it in the Bible, it is always *others* centered. We are to love one another, serve one another, help one another, encourage one another, comfort one another—I could go on and on. It is about getting outside of yourself and deepening your faith by articulating it to others and welcoming others in the name of the Lord.

Going deeper relationally will also broaden your horizons. Not everyone grew up the way you did or had the same kind of parents you did. Not everyone went to the same college you did or had the same hardships you did. You will get to know people who have different perspectives on life—those who can share with you some valuable lessons from their unique experiences. You may even get to know people of a different ethnicity and race.

There are people all around you in your church, neighborhood, and office who have something to offer to you relationally, if you will only reach out and take the risk. Want to do something that really makes an impression on your children? Make a move to deepen your level-two relationships. They will see you sharing your resources. They will see you helping others. And they will understand on a very practical level that that is what God did for us.

ETERNAL LONGING

There is a third level of loneliness that is related to our spiritual loneliness, but it is really a longing unto itself. It is a level-three loneliness that longs for eternity in heaven. Level three satisfaction is reserved for those who have met Christ personally. It is that eternal quenching that will occur when we move from this life into an eternal rest in heaven. This eternal quenching is really the culmination of all of our longings, because it will also ultimately satisfy our level-one and level-two longings forever. We are wired up for a happy ending. Everything in our lives points toward it.

Ecclesiastes 3:11 says, "He has also set eternity in the hearts of men." Because God has placed these eternal longings in our hearts, true fulfillment will occur only in eternity. This is the final hope of people who have placed their trust in Christ. When we are finally home, we will never be lonely again.

Facing Life's Phobias

SPIRITUAL LONGINGS

- But your iniquities have separated you from your God; your sins have hidden his face from you, so that he will not hear (Isa. 59:2).
- "My God, my God, why have you forsaken me?" (Matt. 27:46b).
- At my first defense, no one came to my support, but everyone deserted me. . . . But the Lord stood at my side and gave me strength (2 Tim. 4:16a–17a).
- "And surely I am with you always, to the very end of the age" (Matt. 28:20b).

RELATIONAL LONGINGS

- The LORD God said, "It is not good for the man to be alone. I will make a helper suitable for him" (Gen. 2:18).
- Jesus replied: "'Love the Lord your God with all your heart and with all your soul and with all your mind.' This is the first and greatest commandment. And the second is like it: 'Love your neighbor as yourself'" (Matt. 22:37–39).
- A man who has friends must himself be friendly (Prov. 18:24 NKJV).
- Offer hospitality to one another without grumbling (1 Pet. 4:9).
- "Martha, Martha," the Lord answered, "you are worried and upset about many things, but only one thing is needed. Mary has chosen what is better, and it will not be taken away from her" (Luke 10:41–42).
- Do not forget to entertain strangers, for by so doing some people have entertained angels without knowing it (Heb. 13:2).

ETERNAL LONGING

- He has also set eternity in the hearts of men (Eccles. 3:11).

FACING THE
FINAL FRONTIER

Fear of Death

I ran across a very interesting site on the World Wide Web. It is called the Death Clock.[1] All you have to do is type in your date of birth, answer some pertinent questions about your health as well as your eating and exercise habits, and it will give you your estimated date of expiration.

I was interested to find out that my last day on the earth will be Sunday, December 26, 2034. Hopefully, my death will occur after our 11:45 worship service at Fellowship Church. This Death Clock also informed me that I have about 1.1 billion seconds remaining, and it says that this is the Internet's friendly reminder that your life is slipping away. As if we actually needed another reminder.

This particular clock also gives you some suggestions, based on how you responded to the questions about your health, on how to prolong your life. These include exercising more, eating more fruits and vegetables, and getting the right amount of sleep.

chapter 6

Obviously, I don't believe in the accuracy or validity of death clocks, at least not the ones found on the Internet or any other produced by man. But I do believe that God has a death clock for you and me. He controls my life and death, and only he knows my last day on planet earth. Now, I do believe in eating right, exercising, and getting the right amount of sleep, but I do so to honor and take care of the body God has entrusted to my care. Whether it prolongs my life in any way is in God's hands.

Whenever I deliver a sermon about death, I can sense people shifting nervously in their seats. People generally don't like discussions about death. Even if death clocks were accurate, most people do not want to be reminded that their life is slipping away. We try to ignore death or mask over it by calling it anything but "death."

When someone has died, we say things like: "Their candle has gone out." "He's no longer with us." "She's moved on." "He's gone to be with the Lord." "She passed away; God rest her soul." No matter how we choose to say it, we must face the inevitability of death if we are to conquer the fear of death and live life to the fullest.

The fear of death fuels our modern health movement. Just like the Internet site I mentioned that gave ideas for prolonging your life, a multibillion-dollar health industry has been built upon the premise that somehow we can cheat the inevitable, if only for a little while. Some people have actually deluded themselves into believing that medical technology will some day do away with death and dying all together. They hope and wait in vain for some breakthrough, a proverbial fountain of youth, to eradicate the plague of death.

We pay plastic surgeons large amounts of money for lifts and liposuctions, for tucks and transplants, to reduce and cover over the effects of aging. We supplement our diet of organic foods with a wide variety of vitamins and minerals. We treadmill and triathlon and pump iron, all in an effort to beat the clock. We are trying to beat the odds. We are trying to escape this death date, this expiration date, that we know has been set for us.

Death is total and all-encompassing. George Bernard Shaw wrote, "The stats on death are quite impressive; one out of one dies." I am not going to spend a lot of time trying to convince you whether or not we die. That is a foregone conclusion. But have you noticed how much of our news centers on death and dying. In just one week of news, you are likely to hear of a tragic plane accident that kills everyone on board, the death of a celebrity or sports hero, the tragic murder of children by a disturbed mother or father, the continuing escalation of death in battle-torn countries in the Middle East, or of the death of hundreds, perhaps thousands, in some tragic act of terrorism here at home or abroad.

The list of crimes and fires and wars and calamities goes on and on. About 75 percent of the stuff we see on the news is about death. After hearing or watching the news most nights, I expect the news commentator to say, "And that's the news. We will see you tomorrow evening, if you are lucky enough to still be alive." A friend of mine who attends my church is an anchorman for a local station. He told me, "Ed, in our business, if it bleeds, it leads."

We are going to die. We all know it. Let me elaborate some about what happens the moment after we breathe our last breath here and take in our first breath in the hereafter. What's on the agenda? What's on the Palm Pilot of our lives the moment we graduate from this place and move on to eternity?

The Bible describes in detail the meeting that all of us will have one day after we die. This meeting is going to be huge. The Scriptures describe the players, what they bring to the table, the goals of the meeting, and everything surrounding this event.

Many of us endure a lot of meetings. And when you have a meeting, especially one that is important, you know what is going to happen. You do your homework. You familiarize yourself with what everyone involved in the meeting will bring to the table, the implications and the goals of the meeting.

Amazingly, though, many people are unprepared for the most important meeting in the universe—their postmortem meeting with the Creator of the universe. And on that fateful day their heads will be spinning, and they will be searching for answers. Although the Bible told them in explicit detail what to expect and how to prepare for this meeting, they will be confronted with the sad realization that they ignored God's advice. Many did not do their homework; they did not seek out and apply what the Scriptures said in advance about this time.

For several years I served on the board of trustees at a university. We would have long and drawn out board of trustee meetings every quarter. The agendas were often several pages in length. I enjoyed meeting the people on the board, but my attention span is not that long, and after about two hours I was ready to go. And of course, we would never skip an item on the agenda. Since we only met four times a year, it was imperative for us to address every item on the agenda.

THE RESURRECTION

What's the eternal agenda for your life and mine? What's on the postmortem Palm Pilot? The first item on the agenda, immediately after our bodies die, is that our souls will be transported to an eternal existence in the spiritual realm. What that means for the Christian, the believer in Christ, is an instantaneous trip into the presence of the Lord. Paul tells us in 2 Corinthians 5:8 (NKJV) that for the believer to be absent from the body is to be present with the Lord. For the unbeliever, who will also live on after physical death, the opposite will be true. When they are absent from the body, they will be separated from God in eternity as they await the final judgment (which we will address in the next section). When our candle goes out in this life, it will be ignited in the next life, and we will come back as our true selves, the essence of who we truly are. And that is going to happen immediately after death.

Those who hold to the extinction theory believe, "Once I die, that's it. It is over for me." That is not what God tells us will happen. He says that each of us will move from this life into the next at the moment of physical death. There is life after the grave, and we must prepare for that certainty.

Some think we will be reincarnated. They believe we will stay in some kind of a holding tank for awhile and then be recycled back as perhaps a wealthier yuppie, or maybe as Bill Gates oldest son or something. That's not going to happen. We do not come back to this life in some other form or as another person; our souls move from this life to the afterlife, to an eternal and spiritual state of being.

Maybe you are saying, "Well, Ed, how do you know, how do you really know, there is life after the grave?" If you don't want to take God's word for it, then look at the cycles of death giving way to life in nature. Take a seed, for instance. The seed looks like it is dead. It seems like it is curtains for the seed, but if you plant it the seed germinates and a plant bursts forth. Think about a caterpillar crawling around, an ugly little creature. One day it surrounds itself with a cocoon, which in reality is a tomb, and you think it's history for the ugly insect. Yet one day, a butterfly bursts forth with brilliant color. Notice the cycles of nature, death giving way to life.

The great physicist, Albert Einstein, discovered that matter may change states but it will not be destroyed. Many people who have studied the first law of thermodynamics feel that it is a clue to life after the grave. We will change states, but we will not be destroyed.

Philosophers, also, find a rationale for life after death in logic and in the nature of life and existence. Philosophers have studied human beings and have observed that all of us have a code of ethics, a sense of justice and fairness. Immanuel Kant said this "Since justice is not applied fully, it must be applied in the afterlife by a judge who settles all accounts." The Bible says that God is that judge, and he will mete ultimate justice in eternity.

Anthropologists will tell you that almost every culture and tribe and people group they have studied has an advanced view of the afterlife. Yet the Bible speaks with more authority and more unction than any other book about eternal matters. If you take the words of Jesus regarding eternity and put them up against those of other world religious leaders or gurus, you will see that his words resonate with the conviction of truth.

Also, consider the eight million near death experiences that have been reported. These people experience physical death for a few seconds or a few minutes, and when they come back, they have a completely new and different perspective on life. My grandfather had a near-death experience right after he became a Christian. It changed his life; he was never the same. You may not put much stock in these types of experiences, but if you spend any amount of time around someone who's gone through one, you might just change your mind.

All of these things point to the reality that the soul lives on immediately after death. And then the Bible also tells us that at some point in the future, when Christ returns for the second time, both believers and unbelievers will be resurrected. This simply means that the bodies of those who have died will be reunited with their souls. Acts 24:15b tells us very plainly, "There will be a resurrection of both the righteous and the wicked." The resurrection of the believer will happen first, prior to Christ setting up his millennial kingdom on the earth. The resurrected believer will have a new glorified body and will reign with Christ on the earth for one thousand years in a kingdom of peace, prosperity, and joy. During this time, Satan is bound and unable to wreak havoc on the earth.

The unbeliever who has died, on the other hand, will be resurrected after the millennial kingdom on earth is over. Whereas the body of the believer is raised to honor, the body of the unbeliever, because they have rejected the gospel of Jesus Christ, is raised to dishonor.

It is because of the resurrection of Christ from the dead, and our vicarious participation with Him, as believers, that our bodies will be restored to a glorified and eternal state. What happens after the resurrection, for both the righteous and the wicked, is the next item on our postmortem Palm Pilot.

THE JUDGMENT

After the resurrection of the dead, the believer and unbeliever alike will be judged.

What is the purpose of this postmortem meeting? The judgment—we will be judged. We have a standing appointment to appear before the throne of God. Hebrews 9:27 declares, "Just as man is destined to die once, and after that to face judgment." We live once, die once, and after that comes the judgment of God.

There is no reincarnation, no perpetual cycle of birth, death, and rebirth, culminating some unknown day in an ethereal state of nirvana or paradise. The Bible is very specific about the finality of physical death and the reality, after that, of judgment before the living God.

What is the deciding factor of this judgment? What will be the benchmark by which we are judged on that fateful day during that cosmic courtroom scene with the Almighty? This is the biggest point of spiritual confusion in the universe. The common myth regarding divine judgment is that God will lower the bar. According to this theory, he will ratchet down his holiness, look at the masses, and usher them into their mansions in heaven. The 4-1-1 on the street says that God, being so gracious, will wink at those of us in the middle of the pack, those of us who are basically good people, and say, "Come on into heaven. You weren't perfect, but you tried hard. Welcome to eternity."

Furthermore, the rumor mill continues, "If you are Hussein or bin Laden, a child molester or a serial killer, watch out. You are in the deep weeds. But if you are a good person, if you keep your nose clean, pay your taxes, throw some money to the church or United Way and coach Little League soccer, hey, a good God would not hurl a decent person like you into hell."

Jesus said this common understanding of God's judgment is wrong. The word on the street does not jive with Scripture. Whether

I am a good guy or whether you are a good girl, whether we have paid our taxes, kept our noses clean, whether we have coached Little League soccer—these will not even be brought to the table. It can't be entered into the agenda.

You may say, "I'm Catholic. I was confirmed. I was baptized in a Baptist church. I am in a small group. I am an usher at my church. My grandfather is Billy Graham." That's great. Good for you. But none of these things will be a deciding factor in this cosmic meeting with God.

Have you ever been unprepared for a business meeting? Have you ever been on your heels with your head spinning, grasping for straws? That's the way it will be for a lot of people, because most people are duped into thinking that God grades on the performance plan, that God grades on some national average or a cosmic curve. Not so. God's standard is simply his holiness. His standard of perfection is his very own character. And all of us are sin-stained in comparison to the holiness of God. I am and you are. If we try to face God on our own pitiful merits, we are in severe trouble.

God will be looking for one thing and one thing only in this meeting. He will look at our lives to see if a cosmic transaction has taken place, if we have received what his Son did for us on the cross. That is the final standard by which we will be judged.

We looked at Hebrews 9:27 earlier—"Just as man is destined to die once, and after that to face judgment"—but the thought continues in verse 28: "So Christ was sacrificed once to take away the sins of many people; and he will appear a second time, not to bear sin, but to bring salvation to those who are waiting for him."

Christ came once to die for our sins. We will die once and then, after that, be judged in eternity. When Christ comes again, those who have accepted his forgiveness and committed their lives to him will be spared God's wrath. Those who have not will have condemned themselves by their unbelief.

John 3:16 is perhaps the best-known verse in the Bible. But too often we stop after verse 16 and ignore the rest of the passage in verses 17–18: "For God did not send his Son into the world to condemn the world, but to save the world through him. Whoever believes in him is not condemned, but whoever does not believe stands condemned already because he has not believed in the name of God's one and only Son." God will not condemn anyone to hell on the day of judgment. Those who have rejected his Son and the salvation from sin he has offered to all who believe will already stand condemned on that day. They will have already secured on their own a one-way ticket to an eternity separated from the love of God.

As long as we have breath, it is not too late to appropriate what Christ has done for us on the cross. The Bible says we become a Christian by grace through faith. It is nothing we deserve, nothing we merit. It is simply by God's unfathomable love.

Ephesians 1:13–14 explains the process by which someone makes this transaction and what occurs: "And you also were included in Christ when you heard the word of truth, the gospel of your salvation. Having believed, you were marked in him with a seal, the promised Holy Spirit, who is a deposit guaranteeing our inheritance until the redemption of those who are God's possession—to the praise of his glory."

God's truth is the same today as it was two thousand years ago when Ephesians was written. You have heard the truth of the gospel: the gospel, the Bible says, of *your* salvation. It is a personal thing—of *your* salvation. Only you can personally appropriate the gospel for yourself; no one else can do it for you. And it is my prayer that many who pick up this book will understand the personal nature of the gospel and that they will accept the gift of eternal life that Christ offers.

The passage goes on to talk about "the promised Holy Spirit" as a seal of our inheritance. I love that word *seal* because when we make that defining-moment decision to receive Christ, our very lives are stamped with the person of God in the form of the Holy Spirit. The seal is binding and irrevocable.

This means the transaction is complete and guaranteed until Christ comes back to claim us as his own. If you have been sealed with the Holy Spirit, there is no need to fear your final hour, because death is just a doorway to your final redemption when God claims you as a coheir with Christ.

Here is what happens when we make the commitment to Christ. All of our sinfulness, guilt, shame, and pain are transferred to his shoulders. And all of his forgiveness, love, righteousness, and grace are transferred to our shoulders. That is the cosmic transaction.

Some time ago a friend of mine told me about a Web site that allows you to trade stocks electronically over the Internet. He had to explain to me how this worked because I am doing well just to type my sermons and books on the computer, let alone trade stocks by the computer. I have not invested very much in the stock market, but I thought that it might be fun to put in a little money to see if I could make some money. So I bought a few stocks. When I bought these stocks, the computer screen flashed "transaction complete." It made me feel good to have a confirmed ownership in the company in which I was investing.

What is flashing across your heart today? Does the computer screen of your soul say "transaction complete"? If you have placed your trust in Christ, you are sealed, and the transaction is complete for all eternity. This seal also means that God has taken title to your life. God has purchased us by the precious blood of his Son. We are God's property, and we are his forever. You have nothing to fear; your salvation is secure in the love of Christ.

What does it mean that the Holy Spirit has been given to us as a deposit? The Holy Spirit is still a mystery to many Christians. In our ignorance we tend to discount the importance of this third person of the godhead. Second Corinthians 1:21–22 says: "Now it is God who makes both us and you stand firm in Christ. He anointed us, set his seal of ownership on us, and put his Spirit in our hearts as a deposit, guaranteeing what is to come." We receive Christ, and the seal is placed on our lives. The transaction has been completed, and God has taken title of our lives. Then on top of that the Holy Spirit, the person whom Christ places inside our lives the moment we receive him, is our deposit. In the literal language the word *deposit* means "earnest money."

When our church purchased its land, we had to put up some earnest money. We could not get it back. It was our down payment to show that we were going to pay for the piece of dirt on which our church buildings now sit. When Christ comes into our lives and he places the Holy Spirit inside us, the Holy Spirit is our earnest money.

Do you think that God will not pay in full? Do you think that God will turn his back? The word *deposit* also means "an engagement ring." I love to see single women when they are engaged. They run up to others with their ring finger held high. "Look. Look at my ring. I'm engaged." You can tell they have had their nails done to make that hand look as good as possible.

One of the pictures of the church's relationship with Christ is that of a bride waiting for her bridegroom. Jesus is the bridegroom. The church is the bride. The moment we bow the knee to Christ, he comes into our lives and gives us the Holy Spirit of God, who is our earnest money and our engagement ring. One day the wedding ceremony of the Lamb of God will occur, and the marriage will be consummated in heaven.

Again, this meeting with God in eternity will be about only one thing. Has the transaction been completed in your life or not? At this point you can't take a Mulligan; there will be no do-overs. You can't hire a team of attorneys to defend your case before the judge. Right now the seconds on your death clock are ticking away, and you have had many opportunities to respond to Christ's offer of forgiveness. Have you responded or not? It is not about anything you have done. It is about something you need to receive: "Yet to all who received him, to those who believed in his name, he gave the right to become children of God" (John 1:12).

THE SEPARATION

Let's look at the third item on our postmortem Palm Pilot: the separation. The Bible describes how Jesus will separate all of us into one of two camps. "All the nations will be gathered before him, and he will separate the people one from another as a shepherd separates the sheep from the goats" (Matt. 25:32). We either face eternal bliss in heaven or eternal punishment in hell.

It is impossible for us to fathom what heaven will be like. As an inadequate comparison, take the closest you have ever felt to God in this life. It could have been in a church service. It might have been in a small-group situation or at a summer camp. Perhaps it was while listening to a beautiful piece of music. It could have been while you were walking on a beach or in the woods. Even if you were to take that experience and multiply it many times over, it would still fall miserably short of the glory and the connection we will have with God in heaven.

You could take the best you have ever felt relationally, the closest you have ever felt with another human being, multiply that feeling exponentially, and it will fall miserably short of what heaven will be like. Or you could think about your skills, about a time you were really on a roll using your abilities, and it will fall miserably short of how you are going to use your skills in heaven.

Heaven is also going to be a place, the Bible says, where those who have been separated unto Christ will also have a special bodily transformation. I know many people are looking forward to that. I have already mentioned that both the righteous and the wicked will be resurrected, but the Bible promises that the body of the believer will be raised in glory. First Corinthians 15:42b–44 describes this new body as an entirely different kind than our earthly body: "The body that is sown is perishable, it is raised imperishable; it is sown in dishonor, it is raised in glory; it is sown in weakness, it is raised in power; it is sown a natural body, it is raised a spiritual body."

This passage goes on to say that our glorified bodies will be like Christ's: "And just as we have borne the likeness of the earthly man, so shall we bear the likeness of the man from heaven" (v. 49). Those who have been crucified with Christ by receiving him into their lives will also be raised with him in glory.

Pop culture has not been very helpful in portraying specifically what heaven will be like. What you see in the movies and on television about the little angels flying around with little wings and little trumpets is not a biblical picture of heaven. There will be angels in heaven, but we cannot begin to imagine what kind of awesome creatures they are. As for descriptions of their Creator, our words and imaginations fail us. The apostle John had an awesome vision of heaven and of worship around the throne of God. He recorded these words in Revelation 4:6–10:

> In the center, around the throne, were four living creatures, and they were covered with eyes, in front and in back. The first living creature was like a lion, the second was like an ox, the third had a face like a man, the fourth was like a flying eagle. Each of the four living creatures had six wings and was covered with eyes all around, even under his wings. Day and night they never stop saying: "Holy, holy, holy is the Lord God Almighty, who was, and is, and is to come." Whenever the living creatures give glory, honor and thanks to him who sits on the throne and who lives for ever and ever, the twenty-four elders fall down before him who sits on the throne, and worship him who lives for ever and ever.

The central focus of heaven will be the eternal praise and worship of God. It will be a place of unencumbered worship, unencumbered relationships, unencumbered skill development.

There will be no racism, no backbiting, no wars, and no rumors of wars.

Those who have not been set apart by the Lamb of God for heaven will go to a place called hell. Those people who have not claimed Jesus as their Savior in this life will be separated from him forever in the afterlife.

In their January 31, 2000 edition, *US News & World Report* did a survey on hell. They asked this question: Do you think there is a hell? Sixty-four percent responded, "Yes," 25 percent said, "No," and 9 percent answered, "I don't know." The overwhelming conclusion of the survey was that more people believe in hell today than was true in the 1950s or ten years ago.

The Bible uses several phrases to describe this place. The first phrase used is *outer darkness* (see Matt. 8:12; 22:13; 25:30 NASB). I talk to people who say, "I don't know if I want to go to heaven with all those goody-goody Christians. I want to go to hell so I can 'raise hell' with my friends. We can party in hell." Even if your friends are in hell, you will not know it. It will be like an eternal solitary confinement.

Those who are separated into this camp because of their unbelief will be cast into the outer darkness, or complete isolation. Hell is likely to be a place where all of your sinful desires can come true; you can do anything and everything you have always wanted to do—but utterly and completely alone.

In his book *The Great Divorce*, C. S. Lewis wrote a stunning illustration of what hell represents for the person who has lived only for himself in this life and has rejected God. The premise of this fictional book is that, even if given the chance, the unbelieving person in hell would not want to live in heaven. And on an imaginary bus ride from the depths of hell to the pinnacle of heaven, Lewis shows the great spiritual divide, or the great divorce, that exists between the desires of the believer and those of the unbeliever, and between the false comforts of hell and the real rewards of heaven.

In his introduction Lewis wrote that the book was not to be seen as his personal or theological views on what heaven or hell will actually be like. The purpose of the story was to present a moral or a sort of parable to illustrate that the unbeliever who did not worship God in this life would not be able or willing to do it in the next.

The purpose of Lewis's story was to show that how we spend this life prepares us for eternity. Those who worship God in spirit and truth through faith in Christ will be prepared for the reality of heaven and an eternity spent in the presence of God. Those who worship themselves and live their lives for anything or anyone other than God will be prepared only for an eternity separate from God—in isolation, remorse, and regret.

Here is a description in the story of the mind-set of those who live in hell and their continuing desire to be a world unto themselves: "They've been moving on and on. Getting further apart. They're so far off by now that they could never think of coming to the bus stop at all. Astronomical distances. There's a bit of rising ground near where I live and a chap has a telescope. You can see the lights of the inhabited houses, where those old ones live, millions of miles away. Millions of miles from us and from one another. Every now and then they move further still."[2]

Millions of miles away. This insurmountable distance represents the spiritual state of those who have lived this life only for themselves and will continue to isolate themselves in eternity. They will be separate from

God, separate from his love, and separate from the love and companionship of anyone else, moving further and further into isolation throughout eternity. What a terrible picture of the unregenerate soul.

The Bible also describes hell as a place of *weeping and gnashing of teeth* (see Matt. 8:12; 22:13; 25:30 NASB). It is a place of utter remorse and regret. It will be a place where many people will lament, "I had the chance to commit to Christ. I knew the Spirit was tugging on me. I knew he was pulling on me through that relationship, through that group, or through that church, but I resisted. And now it is too late."

The so-called pleasures of sin and the Evil One, the deceptions of which have kept so many away from Christ, will at last be revealed for what they really are. Misery, loneliness, and sorrow will be the eternal bedfellow of the unrepentant sinner.

Another phrase the Bible uses about hell is "where the worm never dies and the fire never goes out" (Mark 9:48 NLT). Fourth-century theologian Jerome called hell "a place of sensory torment." It is the forever-painful feeling of isolation and separation from God. "But Ed, how could this good God send good people to hell?" You might ask. "How can God slam-dunk this nice family member in my life into eternal damnation? I just don't get it. The God I worship would never do such a thing."

God does not send anybody into hell. We make that choice ourselves. I mentioned this idea earlier in the book. We are made in the image of God, and thus we have been given the freedom to decide our own fate.

Here is what God will do at the end of our existence. He will simply give us in eternity a greater measure of what we desired on this planet. If we bowed the knee to Christ and followed him, at the end of our lives when we have this meeting with God, he will say, "The transaction has been completed, and I will give you in greater measure what you went after on this planet. Heaven is for you."

Conversely, to those who pushed God aside, God will have something else to say. He will say, "You never made the transaction with my Son. I loved you. I sought you. I bought you. I went after you, but you rejected me. You kept your distance from me on earth; you will have a greater measure of this in eternity." We make the choice. God has given us everything we need to believe in him, but he cannot force us to believe.

In the first chapter of the Book of Romans, Paul tells us that God has littered the universe with clues of his existence. All of creation cries out that there is a God, so much so that those who deny his existence are without excuse: "For since the creation of the world God's invisible qualities—his eternal power and divine nature—have been clearly seen, being understood from what has been made, so that men are without excuse" (Rom. 1:20).

Look at the majesty of a mountain range, the placid waters of a forest stream, the intricate features of a newborn child, or the variety, creativity, and color in the flowers of spring. The signs of the Creator are everywhere; they are "clearly seen." Yet some people, in their desperate attempt to deny the existence of God, say that all of this is just an accidental mixing of some necessary organic ingredients in a primordial soup. It is the result of an evolutionary explosion that came out of nowhere, from the hand of no one in particular. There was no first cause, because nothing existed until the building blocks of life came into existence. To quote Paul again, many people are exchanging "the truth of God for a lie" (Rom. 1:25).

God reveals himself to us through many different avenues. In addition to his revelation in nature, he has written his laws on our hearts and revealed himself to us in his written Word, the Bible. He tugs at our hearts. He elbows us. He whispers in our ears. He convicts us of sin, and still so many of us reject him. How can God throw good people into hell? These "good people" have turned their backs on God and in so doing have sealed their own fates.

God is patient, but time will run out. The chances for people to come to Christ will end one day. The Holy Spirit must convict us of sin, but the Bible says that he will not strive with us forever. One of the most chilling texts in all of Scripture is Luke 13:25: "Once the owner of the house gets up and closes the door, you will stand outside knocking and pleading, 'Sir, open the door for us.' But he will answer, 'I don't know you or where you come from.'" The picture Christ is painting here is of a person who has burned up all of his chances. If you think you can do your own thing now and then become a Christian whenever you want, think again.

God is patient, but he will not strive with us forever. How long are you going to test the patience of God? I don't know when God gets tired. He doesn't tell us when he closes the door, but one day the door will shut with many people left stranded in the outer darkness.

I do not want you thinking at this point, *All I have to do is bow the knee and say a few magical words, "Jesus Christ, come into my life." And, poof, just like that, I have a ticket to heaven.* You will miss the train if you think it is that easy. Jesus said, "Not everyone who says to me, 'Lord, Lord,' will enter the kingdom of heaven, but only he who does the will of my Father who is in heaven. Many will say to me on that day, 'Lord, Lord, did we not prophesy in your name, and in your name drive out demons and perform many miracles?' Then I will tell them plainly, 'I never knew you. Away from me, you evildoers!'" (Matt. 7:21–23).

We become a Christian by grace through faith. It is God's will, first and foremost, that we place our faith in Christ and his work on the cross. But a lot of people just say the words without really meaning them.

Just before this passage, Jesus said, "Thus, by their fruit you will recognize them" (Matt. 7:20). The sign of authentic faith is action, the fruit of good works. Am I asking you to doubt whether or not you are a Christ-follower? No. But I am asking you to take inventory. The Christian faith is not some under-the-table deal with God where you can say, "Now I have got a ticket to heaven; I've prayed the prayer. I can do whatever I want and live any way I want. I said the words a long time ago."

If there has been no life change, no discipleship, no growth, God is the judge. But such a lack of commitment should cause one to think. You have every reason to fear death if you have not made a true commitment to Jesus Christ by faith. The old cliché is true: you are not ready to live until you are ready to die. What is written across your heart? Does it say "transaction completed"?

If you have been bought with the blood of Christ, you have nothing to fear. Christ has conquered death. Through our participation by faith in the death and resurrection of Christ, we too can claim ultimate victory: "'Death has been swallowed up in victory' . . . thanks be to God! He gives us the victory through our Lord Jesus Christ" (1 Cor. 15:54b, 57).

In 1876, with the conviction of his faith and assurance of his destiny, Irish minister George W. Robinson wrote these words of hope. May the lyrics of this hymn be yours today as well:

His forever, his alone!
Who the Lord and me shall part?
With what joy and peace unknown
Christ can fill the loving heart!
Heaven and earth may pass away,
sun and stars in gloom decline;
but of Christ I still shall say:
"I am his, and he is mine."[3]

Facing Life's Phobias

THE RESURRECTION

- "There will be a resurrection of both the righteous and the wicked" (Acts 24:15b).

THE JUDGMENT

- Just as man is destined to die once, and after that to face judgment, so Christ was sacrificed once to take away the sins of many people; and he will appear a second time, not to bear sin, but to bring salvation to those who are waiting for him (Heb. 9:27–28).
- "For God did not send his Son into the world to condemn the world, but to save the world through him. Whoever believes in him is not condemned, but whoever does not believe stands condemned already because he has not believed in the name of God's one and only Son" (John 3:17–18).

- And you also were included in Christ when you heard the word of truth, the gospel of your salvation. Having believed, you were marked in him with a seal, the promised Holy Spirit, who is a deposit guaranteeing our inheritance until the redemption of those who are God's possession—to the praise of his glory (Eph. 1:13–14).

- Now it is God who makes both us and you stand firm in Christ. He anointed us, set his seal of ownership on us, and put his Spirit in our hearts as a deposit, guaranteeing what is to come (2 Cor. 1:21–22).

- Yet to all who received him, to those who believed in his name, he gave the right to become children of God (John 1:12).

THE SEPARATION

- "All the nations will be gathered before him, and he will separate the people one from another as a shepherd separates the sheep from the goats" (Matt. 25:32).

- The body that is sown is perishable, it is raised imperishable; it is sown in dishonor, it is raised in glory; it is sown in weakness, it is raised in power; it is sown a natural body, it is raised a spiritual body (1 Cor. 15:42b–44).

- And just as we have borne the likeness of the earthly man, so shall we bear the likeness of the man from heaven (1 Cor. 15:49).

- In the center, around the throne, were four living creatures, and they were covered with eyes, in front and in back. The first living creature was like a lion, the second was like an ox, the third had a face like a man, the fourth was like a flying eagle. Each of the four living creatures had six wings and was covered with eyes all around, even under his wings. Day and night they never stop saying: "Holy, holy, holy is the Lord God Almighty, who was, and is, and is to come." Whenever the living creatures give glory, honor and thanks to him who sits on the throne and who lives for ever and ever, the twenty-four elders fall down before him who sits on the throne, and worship him who lives for ever and ever (Rev. 4:6–10).

- For since the creation of the world God's invisible qualities—his eternal power and divine nature—have been clearly seen, being understood from what has been made, so that men are without excuse (Rom. 1:20).

- They exchanged the truth of God for a lie (Rom. 1:25).

- "Once the owner of the house gets up and closes the door, you will stand outside knocking and pleading, 'Sir, open the door for us.' But he will answer, 'I don't know you or where you come from'" (Luke 13:25).

- "Not everyone who says to me, 'Lord, Lord,' will enter the kingdom of heaven, but only he who does the will of my Father who is in heaven. Many will say to me on that day, 'Lord, Lord, did we not prophesy in your name, and in your name drive out demons and perform many miracles?' Then I will tell them plainly, 'I never knew you. Away from me, you evildoers!'" (Matt. 7:21–23).

- "Thus, by their fruit you will recognize them" (Matt. 7:20).

- "Death has been swallowed up in victory" . . . thanks be to God! He gives us the victory through our Lord Jesus Christ (1 Cor. 15:54b, 57).

KNOW FEAR

Fear of God

I want to share something with you at the outset of this chapter that I rarely talk about publicly. I communicate this to you because a friend of mine encouraged me to do so. I want to confess that I am a fearful man. That's it. I am writing a book about fear and I myself deal with great amounts of fear. In fact, I would call fear a great motivator in my life and work as a pastor. It ebbs and flows in my life on a weekly basis.

This is how fear plays out on any given week as I go about my work as the senior pastor of a large church in the Dallas area. On Mondays I feel a little choppiness on the surface. By midweek the seas often swell from five to seven feet. By the weekend it is as though I am being hit with a tidal wave.

The fear I feel and experience comes from the responsibility of saying something on God's behalf. It is a fear of being a conduit for his truth. Week after week I get extremely nervous and anxious as I prepare and deliver messages from the Word of God. Whether I stood before a congregation of fifteen or fifteen thousand, I would still feel the same way.

On any given weekend, a marriage is teetering on disaster, a family is visiting the church for the very first time, a person far away from God is coming back to the church and investigating again the claims of Jesus Christ, a business person is trying to process a life-changing decision, and someone is dealing with the loss of a loved one. All of these scenarios and more are bouncing around in my head as I speak every weekend. And they are in the frontal lobe of my brain as I write this book—even more so because of the possibility of a wider distribution of my thoughts and words.

Fear drives me to spend an average of twenty-five to thirty hours a week in preparing my weekend messages for Fellowship Church. I know that every six days I have to research, write, edit, memorize, and verbalize a term paper to a wide range of humanity. I know it must be biblical, relevant, insightful, poignant, and interesting. It is not about my ego. Other things may stroke my ego, but this does not. To put it plainly and simply: *the fear I have is the fear of God.*

I know by virtue of sharing this intimate detail about my life with you that you will better understand me and what drives me as a pastor and teacher. But, on the other hand, I know that some people may not quite get what I am talking about. Some just do not connect with this idea of fearing God. But the concept of the fear of God is one of the most misunderstood in all the Bible.

Fear is a very foggy and muddy issue in both life and theology, but I pray that by the end of this chapter the fog will be lifted and the mud will be washed away. If we are to deal with all other fears and have true success in life, we must understand and *possess* a healthy fear of God.

By way of introduction to this concept, however, I think it best that I define for you what I mean by biblical "fear." It is not an emotional quiver-in-your-liver type fear. It is not a bug-eyed, gape-mouthed, screaming-at-the-top-of-your-lungs-with-fright type of fear. God is not a boogeyman waiting around the corner to say "Boo" and scare us out of our minds. The fear talked about in the Bible is simply an understanding of who God is in relation to us. I will explain this further as we go along, but the idea is reverence and awe at the power, majesty, and holiness of God Almighty.

In his book, *Seeing God,* based on Jonathan Edwards's work on evidences of the Christian life, Gerald McDermott writes that a proper understanding of godly fear is one of the evidences of regeneration. A healthy respect for God shows that a person has placed his faith and trust in Jesus Christ as Lord and Savior.

The central idea of the fear of God, according to McDermott, is a fear of sinning lest we grieve the "Savior whom we love." It is founded in a reverence for God or an eagerness to please him. The motivation for avoiding sin is not the fear of punishment but love for God.

Instilling only a fear of judgment or lack of reward does not encourage the proper kind of godly fear that McDermott cites from Scripture. This one-sided understanding of godly fear, I believe, is an immature motivation for living a holy life.

Fear of God springs from hope. And this comes from an assurance of our salvation, of our security in the hands of God because of our faith in Christ. This hope should inspire us to revere God, to love him, and to do what is right for the simple reason that we want to please God, as McDermott reminds us.

The biblical concept of the fear of God is one of those paradoxes of the Christian faith that we may never fully understand until we meet God face-to-face. The Bible couples the idea of fear with the seemingly contradictory quality of joy. Psalm 2:11 speaks of rejoicing with "trembling." And the reaction of the women at Jesus' tomb was one of "fear and great joy" (Matt. 28:8 KJV).

These spiritual ironies are the essence of Christianity. It is, as C. S. Lewis once pointed out, that the stumbling blocks to Christianity and its seeming paradoxes make him believe in it all the more. Somehow, ironically, a biblical fear of God gives us, at the same time, a sense of joy. I defy any other fear to do the same.

As we study further this concept of godly fear, I want to emphasize the idea of balance in the Christian life. Fear is balanced with love, judgment with mercy, accountability with freedom, law with grace, and death with hope. I understand all too well what needs to be done in my life to achieve this balance, but I often find such a balance difficult to achieve.

From making time for private prayer and corporate worship to trusting God with your bank account to balancing evangelism with social action, you may be convicted of many areas of imbalance in your life. But as you trust God, casting aside all other fears, and begin to choose his path, you will experience the peace and satisfaction of being firmly rooted in the things of God:

He will be like a tree planted by the water
　　that sends out its roots by the stream.
It does not fear when heat comes;
　　its leaves are always green.
It has no worries in a year of drought
　　and never fails to bear fruit. (Jer. 17:8)

THE DAD CONNECTION

Proverbs 1:7 says, "The fear of the LORD is the beginning of knowledge, but fools despise wisdom and discipline." In other words, the fear of the Lord is the starting point, the launch pad, for true knowledge. I hope I can say with some certainty that most Christians desire knowledge and wisdom. The Bible tells us in no uncertain terms that we must first have godly fear in order to achieve these godly goals.

One of the major reasons so many people are in the fog and mud about the fear of God is that we get our views of the heavenly Father from the cues we have received from our earthly fathers. Everyone has either grown up in a red-light household or a green-light household, and these different home environments often determine how we view God.

Let me explain. If you grew up in a red-light household, you saw your father as a red-stoplight dad. His favorite word was "No!" You felt like your father's primary role in your life was to stop you from doing things you wanted to do. He halted your wants, desires, and impulses at every turn. And if you ran the red light, the hammer would fall, and he would slap on the handcuffs. Like a household cop, his theme song was, "Bad boy, bad boy, what ya' gonna do?"

If your family of origin was like that, chances are you see God in the same way—unapproachable, always saying "Halt!" or "Stop!" If you run the red light, you expect the hammer of God's judgment to fall and his mercy to be nonexistent. Consequently, you may have come to a point where you have written off God entirely because you have been comparing him with your earthly father. You have said to yourself, "I don't want any part of a God who is anything like my father." You have a fear of God, but it is unhealthy and out of line with what the Bible calls godly fear.

Perhaps you grew up instead in a green-light household. Your father did not have any guardrails or guidelines for you, and it was like living on the Autobahn, where there is no speed limit. "Just go for it," he would say. "It's no problem if you get into a wreck or mess things up. Just do whatever you want." There were no limits to your actions and no consequences when you blew it.

If you grew up in a green-light household, chances are you see God as a green-light God. You do not have any fear of him at all. You think you can do whatever you want and God will not care. There is no such thing as divine judgment because you think God will just let you get away with anything and everything, just like your earthly father. Your fear of God is also not based on a biblical understanding because your fear of him is nonexistent.

Several years ago I talked to a man who was involved in a church, yet he was living a no-holds-barred green-light lifestyle. I could not figure out why he was so reckless with his actions. Then one day he shared with me the kind of relationship he had with his father. It did not take long for me to make the connection between the way his dad dealt with him and the way this man expected his heavenly Father to treat him. He had a green-light dad, and he expected the same liberal treatment from God.

There is yet another kind of household: the yellow-light household. I would say that this type of household describes my family environment, especially as it relates to my father. He was not perfect, and sometimes he turned on the red light too much. But for the most part he gave me the right amount of slack in the rope and pulled it in at the right time. As a result, I think this earthly relationship helped me to have a fairly healthy fear of God. You may be able to identify with me and say, "Ed, I am with you. The relationship I had with my dad really helped nurture in me a proper fear of God."

I must include in this discussion a fourth type of household. It pains me to say that many have grown up in a blacklight household, because they either did not have a father or they had one who was rarely there, either physically or emotionally. You may be in this camp. Your concept of God is really up for grabs because you do not know what to expect from God.

At the very least, you probably view God as distant and uninvolved with your life. For you, and for everyone else who has a skewed view of God because of their upbringing, we need to go on a *fear-finding mission*. We need to spend the rest of this book trying to instill a healthy fear of God in our lives.

A MATTER OF RECOGNITION

If you have not realized this by now, fear is one of the most basic instincts of all God's creatures, including humans. That is why I call the fear of God "Christianity in the raw." The proverb we looked at earlier says that it is the beginning, the basis, of all wisdom. We would do well to look further at how this concept can revolutionize our Christian faith.

First, I want to address what it is about the fear of God that allays all other fears. The Bible says, "There is no fear in love. But perfect love drives out fear, because fear has to do with punishment.

The one who fears is not made perfect in love" (1 John 4:18). The kind of fear that John is talking about in this verse relates to the other fears I have been talking about up to this point. This is an irrational fear—of the future, of commitment, of failure, etc. It also speaks of an irrational fear of God, a fear of God's judgment without an understanding of God's perfect love. In order to understand what it means to fear God in the biblical sense, we must understand who God is and how much he loves us. And we will carry that theme through to the conclusion of the book.

The fear of God is not cowering or tucking your tail between your legs and running away. It is, first of all, recognizing who God is and coming to know his character as revealed to us in his Word. Too many of us do our best Barney Fife impersonation when we think of God.

One of Barney's trademarks on *The Andy Griffith Show* was his tendency to be frightened by just about anything, including his own shadow. When Barney got scared, his eyes would bug out and he would begin to shake all over. He would shake and quake so hard that his gun would fall out of his hands, his hair would start flopping around, and his voice would begin to quiver and crack.

That is not what God wants from us. He wants us to know him and to recognize his power, but he does not want us quaking in our boots with an impulsive desire to run in the other direction. Our reverence for God should draw us to him, not push us away from him. It should drive us to call him by name and to understand better where we stand in relation to him.

One weekend after the worship service, I was shaking hands with the people who were filing through one of the exit doors. I meet a lot of people every weekend, and I enjoy talking with them, brief though it may be. A man walked up to me with his wife and said, "Ed, tell me who I am. Tell me my name." I knew I had met this man before, but I just could not bring up his name in my mind.

Finally, I looked over at his wife and said, "Tell him his name." I have come to realize over the years how important it is to recognize people by name. By singling a person out and calling his name, we are identifying that person in relation to us.

In the same way, we need to identify God as God. We need to tell God regularly who he is and recognize him as the sovereign Lord of the universe. The Bible has many names for God because each name identifies a different aspect of God. These names are important because they communicate to God that we are seeking to know him and to build a relationship with him. God does not need us to tell him who he is; we need to reinforce in our own lives who God is in relation to us.

God is not suffering an identity crisis. He is not saying, "I did not realize I was God. Thanks for telling me. I did not know I had made the heavens and the earth. I am so glad you reminded me that I sent my Son to die on the cross for the sins of the world. Thanks for sharing." No, God does not need this recognition, but we need to recognize him. When I regularly recognize who God is, my pride takes a ride somewhere else, my ego begins to melt, and I realize that he is God and I am not.

I have to remind myself daily that I am a sinner and, if left unchecked, I will go south. And if I do not regularly recognize who God is, if I do not give him that significant slot in my life, suddenly I think I am God. I think I am God ruling over a universe called Me.

And a lot of people I meet these days think they are God. They may not say it, but they do not regularly recognize who God is. They think things and say things like, "I call the shots. I have pulled myself up by my own bootstraps. I have made the money. I am in charge. I will determine my own destiny. I will forge my own future."

We must recognize who God is. Then and only then will we begin to have a healthy fear of God and be able to discern the balance between love and fear.

A BALANCING ACT

Certain things are inseparably linked in our culture: money and Bill Gates, Texas and big hair, chocolate chips and cookies, body piercing and teenagers. Those things are inseparably linked. And so are love and fear in the Bible. Psalm 33:18 reads, "But the eyes of the LORD are on those who fear him, on those whose hope is in his unfailing love." Psalm 118:4 also tells us, "Let those who fear the LORD say: 'His love endures forever.'" Fear and love are part of the balanced equation of God's unchanging character. If you emphasize one over the other, you do not have an accurate or healthy image of God.

When was the last time you jumped on a seesaw? Some time ago I got on a seesaw with one of my twin daughters. She was sitting on one side, weighing in at about 45 pounds. I was on the other with a weight of 185 pounds. If I wanted to, I could have sat down with the full force of my weight on the seesaw and launched her out of the playground. You will be glad to know that I restrained myself, and I positioned myself so that I brought the two of us in balance on the seesaw.

But many of us have an out-of-balance seesaw. We don't recognize who God is, and we don't recognize the critical balance between fear and love. If we fall too far on the fear side, we become legalistic: "Don't smoke, don't cuss, don't chew, don't run around with girls who do." Christianity becomes nothing but rituals and regulations. I must jump through this hoop, I must do this and do that, or else God might hit me with a heavenly hammer. Your red-light view of God starts to kick in: "Bad boy, bad boy, what ya' gonna do?" Christianity is not a legalistic trip; it is a relationship.

On the other hand, we can get the seesaw so far out of balance on the love side that we take too many liberties with God. We think that since God loves us unconditionally, it does not matter how we live. Yes, God does love us unconditionally; but his judgment is tethered to his love. Likewise, our fear of God is a critical component of our love for him. We should obey him because we love him, but a part of that love is a fearful realization that God is an awesome and powerful judge who will hold us accountable for our actions. If we fall too far on the side of love and liberty, we can become lackadaisical about our Christian commitment.

Achieving this perfect balance between fear and love is one of the goals of spiritual maturity. I experienced a similar kind of balance with my earthly father. While growing up, I loved my father. But I also had a healthy fear of him. I have already mentioned my two dogs, Brute and Apollo, in a previous chapter. They also love and fear me. Someone has said that the dog-owner relationship mirrors, in many ways, the human-God relationship.

For instance, I am reminded of an incident with my dog Brute some time ago. At 2:30 in the morning, Lisa and I were jolted out of bed by the earthshaking bark of a mastiff. We waited a few minutes to see if it would stop, but it did not. The barking continued with increased intensity. Lisa turned to me and said, "Ed, something is wrong." So I put on my bathrobe and slippers and walked outside. Sure enough, big ole Brute had gotten out of the fence.

I thought to myself, *I am going to put the fear of God in that dog.* So I marched down that driveway and grabbed him up by the collar. He was still barking. "Brute, shut up. Be quiet," I yelled. I was trying to put fear in this bucket-headed dog's mind.

Then I began to try to drag this huge dog, which weighs about as much as I do, up the driveway. As I was huffing and puffing up the driveway with Brute in tow, my bathrobe almost came off. There I was with my bathrobe half off and my boxer shorts showing, and I was thinking to myself, *What if the neighbors are watching,* "There is Pastor Young in his boxer shorts fighting his dog again." I finally managed to get Brute up the driveway. And this trusting dog, even while he was lumbering along behind me up the driveway, was still loving me.

When I put the fear of God in him, so to speak, it didn't make him run away from me. He was jumping up on me, drooling on me, happy to see me again. He understood who I was as his master and feared me, but all the while he still loved me because of the relationship we had.

When I recognize who God is, I understand that God is God and I am not. This recognition of God as God should cause me to respect his authority in our lives, while at the same time loving him because of his intimate relationship with me as his child.

A MATTER OF ACCOUNTABILITY

Christianity in the raw, coming to terms with the fear of God, is not just about recognition; it is also about accountability. Tax time, April 15, is that date we love to hate. That infamous date represents the time we have to come clean before our government. We have to give an account of our finances, how much we have made and how much of it belongs to the government.

April 15 looms on the horizon every year and brings a few jitters and sleepless nights for most of us. The hassles and headaches of preparing tax forms and then the dreaded thought of writing the big check makes us sweat a little. We can file extensions, go through a number of gymnastics and a lot of rigmarole, but at the end of the day we will have to face the music.

God has an April 15. He has a day of accountability. April 15 influences how I will spend, save, and invest my money. God's April 15, the day of accountability, has a big influence on how I will spend and invest my one and only life. The Bible says that one day I will stand before him and I will have to give an account of every word spoken, every thought processed, every deed done.

If you are a Christ-follower, you will have to give an account before God. I am not referring to punishment. Our punishment was taken on the shoulders of Jesus Christ two thousand years ago. Our sins past, present, and future were forgiven and forgotten. I am talking about a healthy accountability.

The writer of Hebrews talks about the accountability we will face as believers: "Nothing in all creation is hidden from God's sight. Everything is uncovered and laid bare before the eyes of him to whom we must give account" (Heb. 4:13). We must give an account some day, and this healthy accountability motivates me to live a pure and holy life. I still mess up. I strike out, fumble, and stumble. But I am always thinking about that accountability I face for my actions.

Hebrews 12:6 tells us, "The Lord disciplines those he loves." I love my four children in a way that words cannot describe. Because I love them so much, I discipline them. In the same way, God disciplines those of us who are in his family. The moment we become Christ-followers we are adopted into the family of God. The Bible calls it being born again into the family of God. And God is our father, the perfect heavenly parent, who has the perfect balance of fear and love. He will discipline us when we get out of his will. Once again, I am not talking about punishment. Discipline is simply correction driven by love.

One of the areas in which God holds us accountable is how we use the gifts he has given us. Each of us is expected to use his God-given talents and skills for his glory until he returns.

In Luke 12 Jesus told a parable about a master who went away to a wedding banquet and left his servants in charge of the house. The good servants were those who were vigilant and watchful of their master's return. Those who became lazy and derelict in their duties were surprised when the master came home. Jesus will come back like a thief in the night when we least expect it, and we will be required to answer for our unfaithfulness.

Jesus said that those who know their master's will but do not do it will be disciplined for their disobedience. They knew what their responsibilities were, and they knew what the master had given them in order to do their jobs, but they were lazy, disobedient, and unfaithful. Jesus concluded with this admonition in Luke 12:48b: "'From everyone who has been given much, much will be demanded; and from the one who has been entrusted with much, much more will be asked.'"

There will be a reckoning for how we have used the gifts, talents, and resources that God has put at our disposal. Jesus tells us that, in order to show ourselves faithful, we need to make our lives count and to be ready and waiting for his return. Especially during those times when we get tired of waiting and we think he is not coming back, we need to be extra vigilant, because he will return when we least expect him.

I try to live a life that reflects God's character because I do not want to disappoint the Master when he returns and I meet him face-to-face. I do not want to get to the end of my life, look at God on his April 15, and say, "God, I was planning to do your will—some day. I was going to use the gifts you had given me—some day. But I was involved in so many other things. I had all of these other activities planned and fun things to do. I just wanted to enjoy life a little before I got serious about doing what you wanted me to do."

Some day is today. It is time to get serious about taking care of the Master's household until he returns. When God looks at me and asks me to give an account for how I used my gifts and talents, I do not want my life to be riddled with regret. I want the best for myself, and I know you want the best for yourself as well.

Do you want the best for your marriage? I have never met a person who has said no to this question. Do you want the best for your children? Do you want the best for your life? Do you want the best blessings from God? Do you want the best for your finances? Do you want the best for your career? Do you want the best for your future? Do you want the best recreationally? Do you want the best relationally? Recognize who God is and take his accountability in your life seriously, and you will find the best of everything for your life.

A MATTER OF OBEDIENCE

When Moses was at the base of Mt. Sinai after receiving the Ten Commandments, this is what he communicated to the children of Israel in Exodus 20:20: "'Do not be afraid. God has come to test you, so that the fear of God will be with you to keep you from sinning.'" Moses said, *Do not be afraid but fear God.* What kind of double-talk is that? How can fear keep you from being afraid? And how can it keep you from sinning?

We have already talked about the difference between the common phobias in our lives and the fear of God. The fear of God, Christianity in the raw, will keep you from sinning as you begin to recognize that God's love drives his will for our lives. The law that God handed down to Moses was intended to keep Israel pure, to protect them, and to pave the way for the promised Messiah. Out of love he gave them the law, and out of love he disciplined them for breaking it.

What God was saying through Moses was that we should fear nothing else but God. Our love and fear of him will cast out all other fears. Only God is worthy of our awe, respect, reverence, and obedience. When we worship and fear God, nothing else can touch us. And when we understand and connect with God's awesome power, we will be motivated not to sin against him.

Despite their many warnings and the awesome power of God displayed in their lives time and time again, the children of Israel rebelled many times. They disobeyed God and his law repeatedly. They fell into idolatry, drunkenness, and a multitude of other sins. And they paid a price for their disobedience.

The death sentence on idolaters at the foot of Mt. Sinai, the wilderness wanderings, the delayed entrance into the Promised Land, the tumultuous times of the judges, oppression by the enemies of Israel—all these were results of disobedience. When the fear of God was absent, the fear of everything was present. Their fear of God represented trust, and without that trust they had many enemies and hardships to fear.

In his book *Soul Survivor,* Philip Yancey writes about the life of John Donne and Donne's influence in his journey of faith. Donne was the dean of St. Paul's Cathedral in London. His candid work, *Devotions upon Emergent Occasions,* was written during a long illness with the anticipation of death. This book provided for Yancey "an indispensable guide in thinking about pain"[1] and trusting God in the face of death and fear.

Donne experienced much fear during his prolonged illness, particularly a haunting fear of God and his judgment. I want to quote a lengthy excerpt from Yancey's chapter on John Donne. It is a wonderful description of someone moving from an unhealthy, imbalanced fear of God to one that springs from hope, love, and trust:

> Although *Devotions* does not answer the philosophical questions, it does record Donne's emotional resolution, a gradual movement toward peace. At first—confined to bed, churning out prayers without answers, contemplating

death, regurgitating guilt—he can find no relief from fear. Obsessed, he reviews every biblical occurrence of the word *fear*. As he does so, it dawns on him that life will always include circumstances that incite fear: if not illness, financial hardship, if not poverty, rejection, if not loneliness, failure. In such a world, Donne has a choice: to fear God, or to fear everything else.

In a passage reminiscent of Paul's litany in Romans 8 ("For I am convinced that neither death nor life . . . will be able to separate us from the love of God . . ."), Donne checks off his potential fears. Personal enemies pose no ultimate threat, for God can vanquish any enemy. Famine? No, for God can supply. Death? Even that, the worst human fear, offers no final barrier against God's love. Donne concludes his best course is to cultivate a proper fear of the Lord, which fear can supplant all others: "as thou hast given me a repentance, not to be repented of, so give me, O Lord, a fear, of which I may not be afraid." I learned from Donne, when faced with doubts, to review my alternatives. If for whatever reason I refuse to trust God, what, then, can I trust?[2]

Indeed, in what else can we trust if we cannot trust in God? In the paragraph following the above excerpt, Yancey recaps, "In either case he [Donne] would trust God, for in the end *trust* represents the proper fear of the Lord."[3] For John Donne, even his fear of divine retribution was replaced with a proper understanding of the balance between God's mercy and justice. His new understanding of the fear of God came from a trust in God and hope in his inseparable love. He had found a fear "of which [he] may not be afraid," because he knew that by faith he had been placed in the loving arms of his Father, no matter what happened in life or death.

Christianity in the raw is about a willingness to go by God's game plan. It is a willingness to obey, to trust God and do what he says. Solomon, one of the most powerful men to rule over ancient Israel, discovered this important principle too late in life. He was David's heir to the throne, the builder of God's temple, the wisest of kings and the richest. I call Solomon "Solo Man" because he tried to do it his way. For forty years, Solomon tasted power, pleasures, and possessions like we will never experience.

If Solomon constructed his house today, it would probably cost billions of dollars. He had seven hundred concubines. He wrote thousands of proverbs. He was the toast of the town, the man of the hour, too sweet to be sour, the tower of mighty Israelite power. Laymen and leaders alike traveled from far and wide to seek out the wisdom he possessed. Seemingly, he had it all.

Near the end of his life, though, "Solo Man" had many regrets about the years he had spent in hedonistic revelry apart from the will of God. It was during these later years that he wrote the often bitter and sardonic words found in the Book of Ecclesiastes.

After burning up four decades of his life, he looked back in the rearview mirror and penned these words in Ecclesiastes 12:13, which are still so relevant for us today: "Now all has been heard; here is the conclusion of the matter: Fear God and keep his commandments, for this is the whole duty of man."

Solomon had done it all. We could not find a better test case for what it is like to try to live life apart from God and surrounded by all of the pleasures of the world. But after all he had done, possessed, and enjoyed, here was his final conclusion, the net effect of his experiential wisdom: "Fear God and keep his commandments." That, he said, is the entirety of man's duty to God. This is the sum total of all that God requires of us.

God preserved the words, thoughts, and journeys of Solomon so we wouldn't have to take the same meaningless journey that he did in order to come to the same conclusion. Don't spend your life trying all the things the world has to offer, only to come to the end of it filled with regret and bitterness. Take Solomon's word for it now, while you still have an opportunity to redeem the time. Fear God and obey him; that is the conclusion of the matter.

Are you going by God's game plan? God wants willing warriors. He wants people who say, "God, I want to do it your way. I'm not going to be a little god sovereignly ruling over a universe called Me. You are God. I am not. You have the game plan for me that is the best. My life will hit on all cylinders when I fear you and obey you. I want to do what you want me to do."

We don't know what to do unless we know God's game plan. And God's game plan is revealed to us in the Bible. That is why it is so thrilling to know that so many Christians are involved in Bible study classes and small groups. That is why it excites me to know that children are being taught age-appropriate Bible lessons from birth to high school every week in churches all across our country. At Fellowship Church alone over fifteen thousand people show up every week to hear what God has to say through his Word.

All of these things indicate to me that many Christians want to know God's game plan for their lives. Many have discovered that the Christian life works when we follow the playbook. Christianity teaches us the plays we need in order to navigate skillfully through the twists and turns of our messed-up culture.

But some people who are reading these words or who are attending churches week after week are really not in the game. They have not taken the first step to get in the game and understand the playbook. They are going through the motions of religion, warming the benches, but they have no idea about the game plan. Many think they are in the game, but they haven't left the parking lot yet and made their way to the sidelines, let alone entered the game.

You may be saying to yourself, "I thought I was in the game, but I have never made a commitment to God and agreed to play by his game plan." Christianity is a decision followed by a process. You don't just join the process.

Compare the Christian commitment, for example, to being married. You don't just wake up one day and say, "Oh, I'm married. I can't believe it. How did that happen?" Any single person can tell you that it is not that easy. You have to come to a point where you say "I do" in marriage. Then you will understand the implications of the process after that commitment.

A MATTER OF COMMITMENT

The same type of commitment is needed in the Christian life. Have you said "I do" to Jesus Christ? Have you made that once-for-all decision to place your faith and trust in Jesus Christ and his work on the cross? Do you know for sure that you will spend eternity in heaven with God when you die?

If you have accepted this gift by faith, you no longer have any reason to fear death or God's wrath. Christ has taken your punishment upon himself through the death of Jesus on the cross. If you have not done so, please continue to investigate the claims of Jesus Christ from the Bible. The Bible says that there is only one way to God, and Jesus is that way (see John 14:6).

Don't trust in your good works, your church attendance, some religious trip, or "good karma" to get you to heaven. Put your trust in something that is eternal and true, in the person of Jesus Christ, the one and only Son of God, as revealed to us in God's Word, the Bible. God is waiting for you. It's your call.

THE COSTS AND BENEFITS

Christianity is not a complicated thing. People have tried to make it complicated, but it is not. Is being in good physical shape complex? No. It is simple. I can tell you right now how to get yourself into great shape and stay that way. Eat healthy. Do some aerobic exercise three to five times a week. Pump iron. That is all it takes. And while it is easy to explain, I will tell you honestly that it is not always easy to implement. In fact, staying in shape is one of the most difficult things I have tried to do.

The same applies to the Christian life. The basics of following Christ are by no means shallow or superficial, but they are simplistic in nature. The gospel of Jesus Christ is the essence of simplicity, but commitment to him and the continuing process of following him will take everything you have.

The great news, though, is that the benefits of trusting God and devoting your life to him are enormous. No other commitment or area of discipline in life offers the kinds of rewards and benefits that Christ gives to those who follow him. When you make the commitment to him by faith, recognize who God is in relation to you, and submit to his accountability in every area of your life, you will reap all of the great blessings he loves to give his children.

I want to share with you five fringe benefits of a healthy fear of God. Would you like to have direction, compassion, blessings, contentment, and maturity? These are the things God promises to those who fear him.

Direction. We read in Psalm 25:12, "Who, then, is the man that fears the LORD? He will instruct him in the way chosen for him." As we give God his proper place in our lives, we will be more in tune with how God wants us to live. Do you remember the boyhood story I shared earlier about my father carrying me on his back away from the water moccasins? He knew the way home, and he navigated the winding path out of the woods while I buried my face in his back. This is a picture of the person who fears God. When we begin to trust him and deepen our relationship with him, he will make our paths straight.

Have you ever said, "I just don't know what to do?" There have been many times in my life when I did not know which road to take, when I could not see what lay around the bend. But I know the one who does have all the answers, and he wants to share those answers with me. All he asks of me is that I be willing to submit to him.

Christian commitment has no place for pride. God is a jealous God, and he wants all of our devotion. But when we give it to him, he rewards us by guiding and directing us in ways we never thought possible. The assurance of this kind of guidance from an all-knowing, all-powerful, and everywhere-present God should bring us peace of mind. It should chase away any other fears or worries we have in life. We are riding on God's shoulders now, and he has promised to show us the way.

Compassion. When we fear God, we also are assured of his compassion. Psalm 103:13 says, "As a father has compassion on his children, so the LORD has compassion on those who fear him." When we make the commitment to Christ by faith, we are adopted into the family of God. We become God's children. The apostle Paul tells us that we become coheirs with Christ and share in all of the spiritual rights and benefits afforded such a status.

One of those benefits is the unending compassion of our heavenly Father. God shows compassion to the entire world, as evidenced by sending his Son to die for the sins of the world. But God's mercy toward the unbeliever, toward the one who rejects him, will run out some day. His justice will take over and his mercy toward the unrepentant sinner will cease. That person will have sealed his own eternal fate by his unbelief.

For his children, though, God's mercy is unending. Jeremiah speaks of his great hope in the compassion of God toward his people:

> Yet this I call to mind
>> and therefore I have hope:
> Because of the LORD's great love we are not consumed,
>> for his compassions never fail.
> They are new every morning;
>> great is your faithfulness. (Lam. 3:21–23)

This is the hope of everyone who can be called a child of God—that God's mercy will never fail us. Because Christ has already suffered the judgment we deserved, God's justice has been satisfied and his mercy is ours forever.

Blessings. The blessings of God toward those who fear him are many. Proverbs 22:4 (NASB) lists some of them: "The reward of humility and the fear of the LORD are riches, honor and life." The opposite of pride is humility. God has no tolerance for pride, but he rewards humility in both tangible and spiritual ways. Godly fear should bring us to a place of humility before the awesome person of God.

When we commit our lives to God, recognize who he is, and submit to his accountability, we are humbling ourselves before him. And God is a great rewarder of those who live in humility. But the difficult part of humility is that if you think you have it, you probably don't. If you are trying to manufacture Christian humility in order to receive God's blessings, you probably will not find true humility.

Christ taught his disciples the way of humility: "Whoever wants to become great among you must be your servant, and whoever wants to be first must be slave of all. For even the Son of Man did not come to be served, but to serve, and to give his life as a ransom for many" (Mark 10:43b–45).

It is in service to God and others that we become great in God's kingdom. Only in selfless sacrifice, in thinking of others before ourselves, and in making the mind of Christ your own will you find what the Bible calls the quality of humility.

Paul also talks about this kind of humility in a wonderful passage in Philippians 2, which describes the selfless attitude of Christ Jesus. This passage is believed to be a familiar hymn of the early church:

Your attitude should be the same as that of Christ
Jesus:
Who, being in very nature God,
did not consider equality with God something to
be grasped,
but made himself nothing,
taking the very nature of a servant,
being made in human likeness.
And being found in appearance as a man,
he humbled himself
and became obedient to death—
even death on a cross!
Therefore God exalted him to the highest place
and gave him the name that is above every name,
that at the name of Jesus every knee should bow,
in heaven and on earth and under the earth,
and every tongue confess that Jesus Christ is Lord,
to the glory of God the Father. (Phil. 2:5–11)

Christ did not set out on his mission by saying, "I think I will
be humble so God will exalt me." No, he set out to be an obedient
servant, even though he knew that would require his life. As a result,
God exalted him to the highest place.

If you want the riches, honor, and abundant life that God promises, don't look for them. Instead, look for ways to put on the same
attitude that Christ had by being a willing and obedient servant. You
take care of the obedience part; God will take care of the rewards.
By seeking first place, you will be last in God's economy. But by

seeking to be last, by putting other's needs before your own, you will have first place.

Contentment. The idea of being content, of being satisfied with what one has, is a foreign concept in today's world. There is no end to the list of things that we can attain and acquire in life, but very few of these things do we actually need. Psalm 34:9–10 gives us the key to contentment:

> Fear the LORD, you his saints,
>> for those who fear him lack nothing.
> The lions may grow weak and hungry,
>> but those who seek the LORD lack no good thing.

How does the fear of the Lord bring contentment? It is all about priorities. When God has first place in our lives, when we have put nothing else in front of him, he satisfies our every need—because he is all we need.

The new car loses its luster, and the new home does not impress any more. The dream vacation, the jewelry, the clothes, the portfolio of stocks—none of these can compare to the incomparable riches which are ours in Christ Jesus (Eph. 2:7). Godly fear gives us a perspective on life that few people are able to have because it gives us God's eternal perspective on all we do and all we have. Temporal and material things slip in importance when viewed through eternal eyes.

The fear of the Lord also helps us become content because we know that everything we have belongs to God. God has given us just what we need to live, to enjoy life, and to be able to give generously. We understand that all we have is God's anyway, and we are accountable to God for how we use the resources he has entrusted into our care. Instead of hoarding or spending what we earn on frivolous desires, we use our resources to further God's kingdom.

In Philippians 4:12b–13, Paul wrote that he had found the secret to being content: "I have learned the secret of being content in any and every situation, whether well-fed or hungry, whether living in plenty or in want. I can do everything through him who gives me strength." Paul's focus was on Christ, and he realized that regardless of his financial situation, or even where his next meal was coming from, Christ was his security.

That is the bottom line of contentment. Where does your security come from? Paul's security came from his faith in Christ and the knowledge that through famine, prison, beatings, and many other hardships Christ would be his all in all.

When you truly understand who God is and the significance of the relationship you have through Christ, you will know where real contentment lies. The world cannot offer this kind of contentment. Neither can any other religious leader or system. Only Christ brings lasting, eternal peace and contentment.

Maturity. A final benefit to the fear of God is maturity. Over a lifetime of trusting God, revering him, and submitting to his will, we grow into the spiritual maturity that the New Testament calls the sanctification of the believer. This is the process of walking with Christ after making a faith commitment to him. As we follow Christ, we become more and more like him until we win the prize of maturity, the perfection of the saints. Paul described this prize in Philippians 3:

> Not that I have already obtained all this, or have
> already been made perfect, but I press on to take hold of

that for which Christ Jesus took hold of me. Brothers, I do not consider myself yet to have taken hold of it. But one thing I do: Forgetting what is behind and straining toward what is ahead, I press on toward the goal to win the prize for which God has called me heavenward in Christ Jesus. (vv. 12–14).

We will not attain real perfection, of course, until we reach heaven. But Paul is clear that we should press toward this goal and reach for the prize of maturity even in this lifetime. Fearing God brings us closer to the goal as we forge a deeper relationship with him. Psalm 25:14 calls this a covenant relationship: "The LORD confides in those who fear him; he makes his covenant known to them."

God established a covenant with Israel through Abraham, and a new covenant was established through Christ with all who believe in his name. This special covenant is for those who fear God, who trust him. Because we place our trust in him, we receive the confidence of God and the special revelation of his will for our lives. As we trust God with our lives, he trusts us with his will. That is the ultimate reward for godly fear: to have the special confidence of our heavenly Father and to know his plan for our lives.

Fear is the most basic instinct of all creatures. Humans, most of all, have created a myriad of fears, anxieties, worries, cares, and phobias to plague our lives. It is certainly an understatement to say that we know fear. In fact, we know it all too well and experience it daily. But the question that God asks is: Do you really know fear the way I want you to know fear? Do you know godly fear?

When you fear God, you have nothing left to fear, not even fear itself. That is Christianity in the raw.

Facing Life's Phobias

He will be like a tree planted by the water
    that sends out its roots by the stream.
It does not fear when heat comes;
    its leaves are always green.
It has no worries in a year of drought
    and never fails to bear fruit. (Jer. 17:8)

THE DAD CONNECTION

- The fear of the LORD is the beginning of knowledge, but fools despise wisdom and discipline (Prov. 1:7).

A MATTER OF RECOGNITION

- There is no fear in love. But perfect love drives out fear, because fear has to do with punishment. The one who fears is not made perfect in love (1 John 4:18).

A BALANCING ACT

- But the eyes of the LORD are on those who fear him, on those whose hope is in his unfailing love (Ps. 33:18).
- Let those who fear the LORD say: "His love endures forever" (Ps. 118:4).

A Matter of Accountability

- Nothing in all creation is hidden from God's sight. Everything is uncovered and laid bare before the eyes of him to whom we must give an account (Heb. 4:13).
- The Lord disciplines those he loves (Heb. 12:6).
- "From everyone who has been given much, much will be demanded; and from the one who has been entrusted with much, much more will be asked" (Luke 12:48b).

A Matter of Obedience

- "Do not be afraid. God has come to test you, so that the fear of God will be with you to keep you from sinning" (Exod. 20:20).
- Now all has been heard; here is the conclusion of the matter: Fear God and keep his commandments, for this is the whole duty of man (Eccles. 12:13).

A Matter of Commitment

- Jesus answered, "I am the way and the truth and the life. No one comes to the Father except through me" (John 14:6).

The Costs and Benefits

Direction

- Who, then, is the man that fears the LORD? He will instruct him in the way chosen for him (Ps. 25:12).

Compassion

- As a father has compassion on his children, so the LORD has compassion on those who fear him (Ps. 103:13).
- Yet this I call to mind and therefore I have hope: Because of the LORD's great love we are not consumed, for his compassions never fail. They are new every morning; great is your faithfulness (Lam. 3:21–23).

Blessings

- The reward of humility and the fear of the LORD are riches, honor and life (Prov. 22:4 NASB).
- "Whoever wants to become great among you must be your servant, and whoever wants to be first must be slave of all. For even the Son of Man did not come to be served, but to serve, and to give his life as a ransom for many" (Mark 10:43b–45).
- Your attitude should be the same as that of Christ Jesus: Who, being in very nature God, did not consider equality with God something to be grasped, but made himself nothing, taking the very nature of a servant, being made in human likeness. And being found in appearance as a man, he humbled himself and became obedient to death— even death on a cross! Therefore God exalted him to the highest place and gave him the name that is above every name, that at the name of Jesus every knee should bow, in heaven and on earth and under the earth, and every tongue confess that Jesus Christ is Lord, to the glory of God the Father (Phil. 2:5–11).

Contentment

- Fear the LORD, you his saints, for those who fear him lack nothing. The lions may grow weak and hungry, but those who seek the LORD lack no good thing (Ps. 34:9–10).
- I have learned the secret of being content in any and every situation, whether well fed or hungry, whether living in plenty or in want. I can do everything through him who gives me strength (Phil. 4:12b–13).

Maturity

- Not that I have already obtained all this, or have already been made perfect, but I press on to take hold of that for which Christ Jesus took hold of me. Brothers, I do not consider myself yet to have taken hold of it. But one thing I do: Forgetting what is behind and straining toward what is ahead, I press on toward the goal to win the prize for which God has called me heavenward in Christ Jesus (Phil. 3:12–14).
- The LORD confides in those who fear him; he makes his covenant known to them (Ps. 25:14).

"NO FEAR"

Responding to God's Mercy

The common fears of teenage boys are pimples, poor grades, and pretty girls. But one fear towers above all the rest—the fear of not being cool. Coke, Nike, and Nintendo have made millions of dollars by convincing young boys that coolness is just one sip, two strides, and three zaps away. Let's face it, though. Regardless of our age, all of us, in one form or another, want to be known as cool people.

One innovative company, based at Carlsbad, California, stands out in their ability to market "cool" to teens and young adults alike. It markets and sells a line of products called No Fear Gear. They have really capitalized on the current attention to attitude and image in our culture. Their product sells because so many people believe that wearing No Fear shoes, pants, shirts, and hats will make them feel invincible. They will feel confident. And, for boys in particular, they will feel like real men. And this company, like others who sell to our egos, has made millions of dollars selling No Fear Gear. The owners maintain that they are not trying to

chapter 8

get people to do dangerous things but to buy self-confidence and self-esteem.

This line of clothing is not the only place we see the "no fear" slogan today. It has become somewhat of a rallying cry in our bold and individualized society. Courageous Gulf War pilots plastered "no fear" decals on the windscreens of their fighter jets. Cars and trucks careen down the highways with this gutsy statement plastered to their windshields and bumpers. I even saw not too long ago pictures of a house that was about to be submerged with flood waters; "no fear" was spelled out with sand bags on its roof for the press to see. No matter where you go today, you are likely to see these words in some shape, form, or fashion.

Amazingly, while the marketing concept may be new, the sentiment itself is centuries old. I believe the first person who ever modeled No Fear Gear was a man referred to by Jesus Christ in Luke 15. You might know him as the prodigal son. Through the life of this prodigal son, we will observe several stages of this card-carrying, no-fear-wearing, attitude-bearing, individualistic mentality who says, "I bow to no one. And if I do bow, it will be in front of a full-length mirror. I will carve my own course. I will determine my own destiny. I will rule my own relationships."

When we have this kind of no-fear attitude in our lives, we go through four stages with which I think we can all identify. Rather than knowing a healthy fear of God, we live with a reckless attitude of no fear of the Almighty. Based on Luke's parable of this infamous, biblical free spirit, this chapter will identify those stages and relate them to the biblical understanding of the fear of God.

BEHIND THE SCENES

First, let me set the stage for Jesus' story of the prodigal son. The word *prodigal* means wasteful or "reckless and extravagant."[1] Jesus described it this way in Luke 15:13 (NKJV): "And not many days after, the younger son gathered all together, journeyed to a far country, and there wasted his possessions with prodigal living." In other words, this young man burned his inheritance on an all-out hedonistic trip. He tried everything he could until the money ran out. He is remembered as the prodigal son because this kind of wild living characterized his attitude and activity.

The prodigal son was a young man in his early teens, or maybe late teens; scholars are not really sure. It is fairly clear from the lifestyle of his family that he came from a fine Jewish home and had a good father. His older brother was as straight as an arrow—a Jew of Jews. Doing what his younger, wilder brother was about to do never occurred to him as the more responsible son. Our fearless and privileged prodigal son probably attended Palestine private school, was a three-sport letterman, and was set to share in a decent inheritance.

Everything was going great for him, until one day he became aware of a desire deep within. It was a desire that sounded egotistical, almost evil, but he could not shake it off. He heard this voice echoing in the caverns of his consciousness: "Who is in control of your life? What are you going to do about it? Why don't you break free and do your own thing? Don't let your father and his old-fashioned principles hold you back."

At first, I suspect, this young man decided that he was not going to pay attention to that voice, which was telling him to buck authority and to rebel. He probably resisted following these desires for a long time. But day after day, week after week, month after month he heard the voice. And the desires that were ringing in the back of his mind soon found their way to the forefront of his mind.

He was losing the moral battle. On one fateful day he began to obey those desires. One day, Jesus tells us, he walked up to his father and said something like this: "Dad, give me my inheritance now. Give me the Merrill Lynch trust fund, because I want to chase the Middle Eastern dream." His father gave in to his son's wishes. He gave him the cash, the Amex card, and the whole deal. And this card-carrying, no-fear-wearing, attitude-bearing individualist left and went off to the far country to sow his wild oats.

THE DELIRIOUS STAGE

As he began his freefall into sin and recklessness, our prodigal son entered the first stage of a no-fear, godless, rebellious attitude. This is a stage that we all experience at a certain point in our lives— the delirious stage. You might remember this stage as the first time you came face-to-face with the simple fact that sin is fun. You probably realized at this time that if sin were not fun, we wouldn't do it. And like the prodigal son, you might have even indulged yourself for a while in the pleasures of sin before realizing the downside to your self-destructive behavior.

This young man was going against the will of his father as well as living in rebellion before God. In his state of delirium, though, he was either unwilling or unable to come to terms with his own rebellion. He was just having too much fun, enthralled with all the excitement, the freshness, and the tantalizing appeal of things he had never experienced before. You know what I am talking about. There is a certain intoxicating feeling of independence when you go your own way, when you do all the things you've been told for so long that you cannot do.

I had a similar kind of feeling back when I was about sixteen years of age and drove my mother's car alone for the first time. She had a station wagon with a 455 engine beneath the hood. I was driving this big family-mobile all alone down a dirt road with the AM stereo blaring the BeeGees, and I noticed that the sand was kind of loose. The movie *Smokey and the Bandit* had just come out, and I wondered if I could do a power slide on that dirt road. I knew deep down that I shouldn't do something like that with my mother's car, but I felt so free and independent and autonomous. That intoxicating feeling beckoned me on. A voice inside my head said, "Come on, Ed, you are in control now. Don't let your mother and her old-fashioned principles hold you back. Do what *you* want."

Maybe you felt that way when you went off to college for the first time. As a freshman, away from your parents, you could do whatever you wanted to do. Incredible. Or maybe you felt that way the first time you received a bonus check at work. "This is mine. I did it. It is all about me." And then, you set your crosshairs on the most exclusive shopping center in town. And you went into one of those high-dollar stores and bought the first thing you saw. "I'll take it. I did this. This is all mine now." You felt delirious with excitement.

The prodigal must have felt that way. Friends started coming out of the woodwork. He was buying drinks for them at happy hour. He was wearing designer clothes. He was driving a Range

Rover chariot. Everything was perfect for him. He was the consummate playboy with all the trappings and popularity to go along with his new freedom.

THE DESTRUCTION STAGE

But something happened during this delirious stage. As a result of his reckless and carefree living, he began to get into trouble. Before the prodigal son realized it, the delirious stage was quickly metamorphosing into the second stage: the destruction stage. The Bible says that after we are delirious with excitement, after we have experienced those intoxicating feelings of independence, it is just a matter of time before we feel the effects of our self-destruction taking place.

The destruction stage of this young man's life is recorded in Luke 15:14–17. Verse 14 marks the transition into this stage: "After he had spent everything." This young man was trying to leave home to find himself, but he lost himself. He had spent everything. His resources were burned out. The friends were gone. His clothes were tattered. He was in a heap of trouble. Sin is like that. Sin promises success but ends in failure. Sin promises freedom but delivers slavery. It looks so good and so right, but the destruction phase is brutal.

Verse 14 tells us, "After he had spent everything, there was a severe famine in that whole country, and he began to be in need." Have you ever felt like you were in need relationally, spiritually, or financially? Any one of those needs, on its own, is a tough situation. The prodigal son was experiencing need on all of those fronts at the same time. He was at the very lowest point in his life. He was alone.

He was spiritually bankrupt, and he was financially wiped out. We are talking about dire need here.

Then, the Bible says, this young Jewish man did something that was detestable, that was the lowest of the low for a Jew to do: "He went and hired himself out to a citizen of that country, who sent him to his fields to feed pigs" (v. 15). Jews believed that pigs were unclean. Here was the prodigal son—the man who had the Range Rover chariot that was broken down, the man who had the designer clothes that were all tattered, the man who had the flashy jewelry that he had to sell to the pawn shop—working with pigs. The Bible says he wanted to eat the pods that were being fed to the pigs. In other words, he was trying to elbow out Arnold Ziffle for some of his slop. In the mud and the mire of a pigsty, the prodigal had gone, that quickly, from the pinnacle to the pit.

Verse 17 of Luke 15 is one of the classic verses of the Bible. In the King James Version the text says that he "came to himself." But the text of the New International Version says, "When he came to his senses, he said, 'How many of my father's hired men have food to spare, and here I am starving to death!'" An empty stomach has a way of preaching to us. He was beginning to smell from the stench of the pigs. He looked at himself, and he couldn't believe what he had done. He knew that his father's servants had it better than he did. And he began to feel bad about himself. Jesus said that he "came to his senses," or he woke up and smelled the pig slop, so to speak.

The Old Testament writer of Proverbs 14:12 understood well the principle Jesus was trying to get across with this New Testament parable: "There is a way that seems right to a man, but in the end it leads to death." When the prodigal son "came to his senses," he realized that he was dead wrong. He had frittered away his inheritance and lived for a time in reckless abandon because he thought this would give him freedom and independence. He was wrong. It did not give him freedom; it brought him instead into bondage and ruin.

The lesson in Proverbs and in Jesus' parable is one that mankind still has not learned. We continue to try to do what seems right to us, to take the reins of our lives, but our finite and feeble understanding apart from God will lead us into ruin every time.

A couple of years ago about forty people from my church, including myself, boarded a Lufthanza 747 flight to the Middle East. A 747 is a huge and complicated plane to fly, I am sure. What if I took a seven-year-old boy—for example, my son, EJ—and escorted him in my car to DFW airport. What if I then put him in the captain's seat of that Lufthanza 747 jumbo jet and told him, "EJ, fly the plane. You can do it, boy. Come on, show me what you've got."

There is no way a seven-year-old boy can fly a 747 because he is ill-equipped for the job. But this is what God must be thinking about us when we try to commandeer our lives and do life apart from his control, his wisdom, and his expertise. When we do this, we are thumbing our noses at God. We are putting on our No Fear Gear, jumping into the cockpit, sitting in the captain's seat, white-knuckling the throttle and saying, "God, I am going to fly this plane. I'll determine my altitude. Thank you very much, but I don't need any flying lessons. I can fly this baby on my own."

When we do that, when we exhibit that card-carrying, no-fear-wearing, attitude-bearing, individualistic mentality, it is just a matter of time before we crash. It is not *if*; it is *when*. EJ will crash if he tries to fly a 747. I am going to crash, and you are going to crash if we do life away from God. God is standing aside saying, "Let me fly. Your craft is custom-made to be flown by me. Won't you let me sit in the captain's seat of your life?"

But we say, "No thanks, God. I know how to handle this marriage problem alone. I know what to do in this dating relationship. I know what to do financially. I know how to invest this money. I know how to move or buy that house. I know what to do all on my own. The only bowing I am going to do, God, is before a full-length mirror. Thank you." Many people will meet God face-to-face one day and will have to say to him, "God, the theme song for my life was 'I Did It My Way.'" This was the theme song of the prodigal as he crashed into the destruction stage of his rebellious lifestyle.

THE DECISION STAGE

The third stage is another that we all go through. Whether outside or inside the family of God, we all experience this stage I call the decision stage. The prodigal had a choice to make. He had two options. The first option was for the really hard-core, card-carrying, no-fear-wearing, attitude-bearing individualist. Here is what he does. After he has crashed, and even after the black box has been recovered revealing that he crashed because of his self-centeredness, he says, "Well, I will lick my wounds. I can fix everything. I still believe I can do it myself. I will crawl back into the cockpit of my life. I will sit in the captain's seat again. I will rebuild and fly this plane again."

He crashes again, recovers the black box again, listens to the reason for his crash again, and begins to fly his own life again. The same thing happens repeatedly. There are piles of wreckage everywhere. That is the price that the card-carrying, no-fear-wearing, attitude-bearing individualist is willing to pay. "I am not going to submit to the Scriptures, God. I am not going to submit to you, God. I am not going to submit to my spouse, God. I am not going to submit to my accountability group, God. I will do it myself, thank you." That is the first option.

The second option we have is to do what the prodigal son did. We can make an assessment of the situation. We can look at the wreckage and say, "This is nuts. What am I doing? I must come to my senses." This is what the prodigal did in Luke 15:18. "I will set out and go back to my father and say to him: Father, I have sinned against heaven and against you." He was already rehearsing what he was going to say to his father. He was in the mud, muck, and mire. Not only was he feeling bad; he was also saying, "OK, I will set out, I will go back, and I will say to my father that I have sinned."

He didn't offer excuses for why he did what he did. He didn't say, "The reason I did this was because I didn't receive counseling as a teenager." He didn't say, "The reason I did this was because I came from a dysfunctional family." He called sin what it was. And then "he got up and went to his father" (v. 20). Some of us need to get up out of that relationship. We need to get up out of that business deal. We need to get up, turn toward God, and come home.

As I rub shoulders with Christians at various places in their journey, I see many people who appear to want God to be the director of their lives. But if the truth were known, beneath the veneer, beneath the exterior, beneath the facade, many Christians are wearing a "no fear" shirt. Their arms are crossed defiantly as they mutter under their breath, "I run this life."

I challenge you to do something. I challenge you to uncross your arms, to open your palms toward heaven and say, "God, have your way in my life." Have you done that? The prodigal did that.

THE DELIVERANCE STAGE

And now we move to the fourth stage. Before I address the fourth stage, I want to tell you something. All of us, no matter where we are from, go through the first three stages. The fourth stage, though, is only reserved for those of us who have guts, those who really want to have Christ enter into the picture and deliver them fully and totally and completely. The fourth stage is the deliverance stage.

If you make the decision to come to your senses, to go in the opposite direction of your sinful rebellion, to repent and turn toward the father, you are in the process of being delivered. And here is where the plot thickens and it gets really exciting. The latter half of Luke 15:20 reads, "But while he was still a long way off, his father saw him." This may seem like an insignificant part of the story, but it is really an amazing testimony to the father's love for his youngest son.

The father had obviously been waiting for his son to return. He had been watching, looking in the distance, and waiting for him to come home. He might have been going up on the rooftop every day for the past couple of years on the slightest hope that he might see his son making his way home again. Or perhaps it was his habit to stand at the edge of their property and stare down the road in anticipation of his son's return. The Bible says he saw him from a distance and that he knew it was his son.

How did this old man recognize his son from that far away? They didn't have contact lenses or glasses back then. How did he do it? I'll tell you how I think he might have recognized him. When I was a teenager, my father was a long way off from me while I was fooling around with a group of kids. I didn't think he knew I was with the group.

Suddenly, I heard this voice say, "Ed, come here."

I looked up. My father can't see very well. I ran over and asked, "Dad, how did you know it was me?"

He said, "Ed, by your walk." I have a unique walk, so my father was able to identify me as his son.

When our heavenly Father sees us take that most difficult first step, he recognizes us at once. "That is my boy. That is my girl. I recognize their stride. They are mine." In a similar way, I believe, the father of the prodigal recognized his son from a distance.

The text continues, "His father saw him and was filled with compassion for him." We matter to God even with the mire and the mud and the crud all over our lives. You are still a much-loved person by God. But here is the real kicker. "He *ran* to his son" (v. 20, emphasis added). The father saw his son from a distance and ran to meet him, to welcome him back. The word *ran* in the Greek language is a powerful, life-changing word. Let me explain briefly the cultural meaning behind what this man did.

Middle Eastern men never ran. It was unheard of for them to run, especially for a wealthy, respected, and elderly landowner like this man. Yet this father ran and greeted his son. The Bible also says that he embraced his son. The law, specifically in the Book of Deuteronomy, demanded that this young man, who took the Merrill Lynch trust fund and squandered it on reckless living, this prodigal, this card-carrying, attitude-wearing, no-fear-bearing individualist should have been stoned by the neighbors.

If the neighbors, though, had stoned the son, they would have had to stone the father as well. Why? The father was just as culpable because the father was embracing the son and welcoming a sinner back home. What a picture of what Jesus did for us on the cross. He embraced us. He took the licks. He took the hit for our sins. He is a compassionate, loving, and gracious God who wants to know us, who wants to relate to us, who wants to lift us up in his arms and draw us near to him.

Luke 15:20 concludes, "He ran to his son, threw his arms around him and kissed him." The Bible then says that they had a giant party. The prodigal son was trying to get his rehearsed confession out. "Dad, I have sinned against you. I am sorry." His father, though, had already forgiven him and was ready and waiting to welcome him home. He was so excited that he took this son to the Gap, bought him two outfits, and had some Domino's Pizza delivered. That, at least, is my modern-day interpretation of what happened. In short, they had a party. It was a coming-home extravaganza.

Here is how Jesus describes the father's response to his son's homecoming, beginning in verse 22 and continuing through verse 24: "But the father said to his servants, 'Quick! Bring the best robe and put it on him.'" Only family members wore robes. "Put a ring on his finger." This phrase describes the family signet ring, the power of attorney, that was used to seal documents. "And sandals on his feet." Only family members wore shoes. If you were a slave, you didn't wear shoes. "'Bring the fattened calf and kill it. Let's have a feast and celebrate. For this son of mine was dead and is alive again; he was lost and is found.' So they began to celebrate."

You might be thinking, "You mean this father put on this kind of party for the son who had rebelled against him, who had done his own thing and wasted his inheritance?" Yes, and that is the kind of party God wants to throw for us when we turn back to him. But, again, we are back to this issue of consequence. We are back to the issue of confronting our no-fear mentality. If you are honest with yourself, you may find that you are paying high tabs for this card-carrying, no-fear-wearing, attitude-bearing, individualistic mentality that says, "I'll do my own thing."

You may be paying high tabs in relationships, because you have burned through a marriage or two. These, in turn, may have brought about negative circumstances for a child or two. Maybe spiritually you still want to cling to your own notions about what saves a sinner instead of trusting in what God says saves a sinner. Maybe financially you have bought into the lie that more is better and better is more, and you are up to your eyeballs in debt. You may not look like it from the outside, but you are. You can't even give God the 10 percent to the local church that he asks of you.

If I were God (and you should be glad I'm not) and I had people running around in these No Fear T-shirts, blowing smoke toward heaven and saying, "I'll do my own thing," I would blow smoke right back. My motto would be, "Too bad, so sad." But God doesn't do that. Even though we blow smoke at him, we still matter to him. He still loves us more than we can even comprehend. And he is waiting for us to make just a little move to reverse our field spiritually so he can come running to greet us and save us and change us and restore us to his family. We can wear his robe, put on his ring, and wear his shoes. But the choice is up to us.

Who is flying your craft? Are you flying it? If you are, I will tell you point blank that it is bound to crash. When you recover the black box and replay what you find there, you will have a decision to make. Will you continue on a flight path of recklessness, finding yourself in crash after crash? Or are you now going to say, "God, I am tired of crashing. I want you to fly my craft?"

What kind of posture are you exhibiting today? Who is on the throne of your life? Are you all decked out in No Fear Gear? Isn't it about time that you uncross your arms, open your palms toward heaven, and say, "God, I have tried to do it my way. Have your way in my life." Can you say that in every area? If you can't, make a decision to do it today.

Facing Life's Phobias

THE DELIRIOUS STAGE

- "And not many days after, the younger son gathered all together, journeyed to a far country, and there wasted his possessions with prodigal living" (Luke 15:13 NKJV).

THE DESTRUCTION STAGE

- "After he had spent everything, there was a severe famine in that whole country, and he began to be in need" (Luke 15:14).
- "So he went and hired himself out to a citizen of that country, who sent him to his fields to feed pigs" (Luke 15:15).
- "When he came to his senses, he said, 'How many of my father's hired men have food to spare, and here I am starving to death!'" (Luke 15:17).
- There is a way that seems right to a man, but in the end it leads to death (Prov. 14:12).

THE DECISION STAGE

- "'I will set out and go back to my father and say to him: Father, I have sinned against heaven and against you. . . . So he got up and went to his father" (Luke 15:18, 20a).

THE DELIVERANCE STAGE

- "But while he was still a long way off, his father saw him and was filled with compassion for him; he ran to his son, threw his arms around him and kissed him" (Luke 15:20b).
- "But the father said to his servants, 'Quick! Bring the best robe and put it on him. Put a ring on his finger and sandals on his feet. Bring the fattened calf and kill it. Let's have a feast and celebrate. For this son of mine was dead and is alive again; he was lost and is found.' So they began to celebrate" (Luke 15:22–24).

A MYSTERY REVEALED

Our Hope in Christ

If we were to take a survey today among Christians and everyone responded with complete honesty and candor, I believe we would discover that many in the church feel as though they are in hopeless situations. You may be one of those people. You may feel hopeless about a marriage that is not getting any better. You may feel hopeless because you are not yet married and don't have any prospects in the foreseeable future. Maybe you are a husband or wife who feels hopeless because you don't have a child yet. Or maybe you feel a sense of hopelessness because of a difficulty at work, a financial setback, or a debilitating illness.

In the midst of all the fears we are likely to face in this lifetime, hopelessness is a pervasive condition in the world today. But the Bible gives us the secret for being hopeful. The secret is revealed to us in a little book called Colossians. In Colossians 1:26–27 Paul says that a mystery has been hidden for ages but has now been revealed. And this mystery, this secret, is revealed to the saints of God, even the Gentiles: "Christ in you, the hope of glory." Note the phrase "in you." If we are in Christ, Jesus gives us the reason for hope. And this

chapter 9

is precisely why, if you are a Christ-follower, you should be among the most confident and most hopeful people on the planet.

This chapter will ask the question: How do I have a hope that never hides? Even when our fears seem to engulf us, when we can't seem to find a reason to hope, how do we tap into that source of hope that lives inside us as Christ-followers? The world says that hope is fate, crossing your fingers. It is good luck. It is knocking on wood. The Bible, on the other hand, says in Colossians 1:27 that hope is a person. Because of the unfailing character of the person of Christ, we can be confident that what he says and what he promises will actually happen. That is biblical, honest-to-goodness, Holy Spirit-inspired hope. Do you have that kind of hope?

Every time I think about hope, my mind rushes back to an occasion several years ago when Lisa and I were planning to take a mission trip to the Orient, specifically Korea. This mission trip was really exciting for us, but we were hesitant about leaving. Our oldest daughter LeeBeth was only three years old at the time, and we had not been away from her for an extended period of time. We did decide to make the trip and entrusted LeeBeth into the care of loving relatives. We kissed LeeBeth goodbye and hugged her, and Lisa got a little teary at the prospect of leaving her little girl for two weeks.

As we turned to walk to the car that was taking us to the airport, LeeBeth said, "Mommy, Daddy, please bring me back a Korean outfit." Now is that classic, or what? This is the typical toddler response when mommy and daddy leave for a trip: bring me back a present. We promised that we would try our best to do just that.

We went to the airport, hopped on the plane, and made it safely to Korea. We spent two incredible weeks there and then made our way back. When we pulled the car in front of the house and walked up the walkway, the door flew open, LeeBeth ran out, jumped into our arms, kissed us, and said she was so glad we were home. Then, without missing a beat, she said, "Put me down. Put me down." We did as she asked, and she immediately began to take off her clothes. We were startled and asked what she was doing taking off her clothes outside, in front of the neighbors.

She responded excitedly, "Where is my new outfit?" We unbuckled our suitcases, took out the Korean outfit, and gave it to her. And she put it on. Now that is hope! She was confident in what she expected to happen because her hope had been placed in her mommy and daddy, who promised it would happen.

Over the next several pages, we are going to look at one of the greatest passages in the Bible: Romans 8. This passage outlines for us several reasons why we can be people of hope. In other words, it gives us the benefits of having Jesus Christ in us. I think it is safe to say that many people who are in Christ, who call themselves Christ-followers, who are born-again people, take for granted the incredible benefits they have. As Christians, many of us don't realize what we have in Jesus Christ.

You may be reading this book right now as a person who is checking out this Christian thing. You may be at a place in your life where you are investigating Christianity. If you are a seeker, someone who is searching for answers, that is great. I pray that this book can help you find the answers you seek about Jesus Christ and what he can do in your life.

But I want to communicate right up front that the concepts in this chapter are primarily for those of us who know Christ personally.

If you are seeking, if you are investigating the Christian life, please keep reading. I hope you can begin to understand the great deal that is being offered to you, if you will give your life completely to Christ. So continue to read very carefully, think about and contemplate this great hope that Christians talk about—this hope that never hides.

I Have Been Pardoned

The first reason we should be hopeful is that we have been pardoned. I should have confidence in what it is to hope in the person of Christ because I have been pardoned. The Bible says this in Romans 8:1 (TLB), "There is now no condemnation awaiting those who belong to Christ Jesus." Notice it did not say there are now no mistakes, there are now no failures, or there is now no sin. It says that there is no condemnation.

All of us mess up. Even the legendary leaders of the faith took a tumble now and then. Abraham lied about his wife. David committed adultery with Bathsheba. Simon Peter denied knowing Christ three times in one night. Moses struck the rock in anger. None of these people experienced or suffered condemnation. But they did experience the consequences of sin. This is a key distinction in the Christian life. We are destined to come face-to-face with the consequences of our sin but not condemnation for our sin.

You may have heard something similar to this as a child, or perhaps you have said this to your own children: "I am not going to punish you, but you will have to suffer the consequences of your actions." The whole world still groans under the consequences of what Adam and Eve did in the Garden of Eden. Even though God, through Christ, has provided a way for us to be forgiven of sin, we still have to face the inevitable consequences of our sins and the sins of those who came before us.

In his letter to the Galatian Christians, Paul warns us that sin brings forth a harvest of destruction: "Do not be deceived: God cannot be mocked. A man reaps what he sows. The one who sows to please his sinful nature, from that nature will reap destruction" (Gal. 6:7–8). When we make sinful choices, we are sowing seeds that will yield a crop of miserable consequences. God forgives, but he does not remove the inevitable fallout from our poor choices. He may choose to do that sometimes, but he will generally use the consequences of sin to teach us the joy of a spiritually disciplined life.

While we may have to deal with sin's consequences for a time, the great news is that there is no eternal condemnation for those who are in Christ. This word *condemnation* means punishment. We are never going to be punished for our sins if we are in Christ. Did you catch that? I will repeat it one more time. We are never going to be punished for our sins if we are in Christ. Is that good news, or what? Talk about a benefit. That is unbelievable. Christ takes the penalty for our sin, when we personally receive what he did for us on the cross. And we are forever free from God's wrath, the righteous judgment of God for sin.

In a real sense the world is on death row. I have visited people in prison, and I have seen death row. It is a depressing place. The men and women there are condemned to die by a duly appointed judge because they have done something deserving of death in the eyes of the law. Because sin entered into the world through Adam, we are all born sinners and condemned to die by the judge of the universe. All of us are unrighteous before a holy God. And all humanity finds itself on death row. But the great hope of the believer is that God loved the world so much, even while we were on death row, that he sent Jesus Christ to take the death penalty for our sins. If we have received that, we have been pardoned. We have been set free.

The Bible says in Hebrews 7:19b (TLB), "But now we have a far better hope, for Christ makes us acceptable to God, and now we may draw near to him." You already know as a Christian that you have accepted Christ, but do you realize that God has accepted you because you have been pardoned? And as a result of this pardon, we may draw near to him. We have access to the throne of God through the blood of his Son. We have been given the benefit of Christ's righteousness through faith. When he looks at us, God accepts us as clean, pure vessels. The Christian life would be worth it, even if there were no promise of eternity in heaven, just to have a clear conscience before God.

One of the major causes of hopelessness is shame and guilt. The Evil One likes to stuff our pockets full of shame and guilt, even though he knows that we no longer stand condemned before God. He wants us to forget that we have been freed from punishment. He wants us to live in constant fear of the wrath of God so we will lose our effectiveness as disciples. When we are still living in bondage to sin, we are not able to be effective witnesses for Christ and to experience the freedom we have in the Spirit.

Satan often whispers to us, "You are going to be punished for that. God will get you back for that one. He is going to hammer you. You had better look over your shoulder because one night you will be walking down the street and God will come up behind you and punish you." Those are lies, Christian. Satan is a liar. He is the father of lies and the greatest liar in the history of the world. He has been lying for thousands of years, and his strategy is to keep Christ-followers hemmed in and limited.

Satan works hard at keeping many of us who are in Christ in a state of hopelessness and fear. He whispers lies to us day in and day out. "You can't do that because of your past." "God can't use you any more because of what you did last week or last month or last year." We must call him a liar and remember that we have been pardoned. We will suffer consequences, but we are not condemned. Christ took the punishment once and for all. It is over, signed, sealed, and delivered. Now we can go on and live our lives. We have an everlasting pardon from the divine judge of the universe.

WE HAVE THE POWER TO CHANGE

The second benefit of being a believer is that we have the power to change. Simply by being plugged into Jesus Christ, we have the power to make life-altering changes, to become better people, to break free of the sin that entangles us. You may think that all people have the power to change within themselves, whether they are Christians or not. Everyone can make changes to some degree. But these are superficial and temporal changes that have nothing to do with the real inside-out kind of transformation that Christ offers. Only he can change the heart. Only he has power over sin and death. Only he can make us perfect by remaking us into his image.

A few years ago I took a stress test. The treadmill was plugged into an electrical outlet, and there was a technician on one side and a doctor on the other. I stepped up on the treadmill, and they started it. It moved slowly at first, then faster and faster. The incline began to increase higher and higher. I was worn out after about twenty-five minutes, sweating profusely and gasping for breath. My legs began to feel very heavy, as if I no longer had the strength to lift my feet off the treadmill's belt.

The doctor said, "Mr. Young, any time you want to stop just give me the nod, and I will push the stop button."

I did not hesitate to respond, "I'm nodding, I'm nodding."

He stopped the treadmill and I got off. I felt so much relief. I felt such freedom finally to be off that incessantly turning belt. In a real sense, human beings are on a treadmill called sin and death. And here is the cycle. Here is how the belt turns on this spiritual treadmill: We are tempted, we fall, we feel guilty.

The incline gets ratcheted up in an unhealthy relationship, the belt begins to turn faster in a damaging habit, and the treadmill just keeps going. In desperation we begin to realize that something is wrong inside and we don't really have the power to change that we thought we had. We say, "I can't change. I am powerless to change. I don't have anyone who can help me off this treadmill." But if you are in Christ, you do.

Paul tells us about this power in Romans 8:2 (TLB), "For the power of the life-giving Spirit—and this power is mine through Christ Jesus—has freed me from the vicious circle of sin and death." Whatever has control over you, whatever you are dealing with, if you know Christ personally, turn to him and nod. Tell him that you are tired, your legs are getting heavy, and you want to get off the treadmill. If you are in Christ, you are plugged into his power, and you can ask him to give you the strength to take care of whatever difficulty you may be experiencing. And he will do it. Jesus Christ has freed us from the vicious cycle of sin. That is the second benefit of being a believer.

WE HAVE A PURPOSE FOR SUFFERING

The third benefit of the Christian life is that we have a purpose for suffering. We have been pardoned. We have the power to change. And we have a purpose for suffering. The Bible says we will suffer. God does not promise an exemption from pain and suffering in the Christian life. James 1:2 is quite clear on this: "Whenever you face trials of many kinds." The text does not say "if" but "when." Suffering is inevitable.

Life is full of problems. I know this is not a particularly profound statement. You know this as well as I. You are most likely either in the middle of a problem, coming out of a problem, or preparing for the next problem. That is life. It is easier to deal with the problems we face if we know that there is a greater purpose for them. The thing that really gets us down is when a problem occurs in our lives and we don't understand its meaning.

I am like the guy in the back of the classroom with his hand up and frantically waving for attention. "Oh, God, choose me. I don't understand. You are going too fast, God. Please choose to answer my questions." On the other hand, if I see a purpose behind the prolem, if I see a purpose to suffering, then I respond, "Aha, now I understand it. That's why God is doing this in my life." I can trust that God is allowing certain things to happen for a greater purpose.

The Bible says that if we are in Christ, we understand and know the purpose behind suffering. Romans 8:28 is a popular verse for Christians: "And we know that God causes all things" (NASB). Circle the phrase *all things*. God is working in the midst of everything that happens, both good and bad. Does that mean divorce? Yes. Does that mean death? Yes. Does that mean a financial setback? Yes. Does that mean the loss of a job? Yes. Does that mean a relational breakup? Yes. Does that mean a relocation? Yes. He uses all things, good and bad, for a greater purpose. He does not intentionally cause bad things to happen to us, but he is able to use the problems of this fallen world for his glory and our growth.

A lot of people blame God for things that he shouldn't be blamed for. We live in a fallen world because God created us with the freedom to choose right or wrong. From the very beginning, mankind has had a choice to follow the Lord or not. And, from the beginning, we have chosen to do wrong. Many of the negative experiences that we face in life are due to the fact that we have made incorrect choices. But we love to point the finger of blame at God when things go wrong in our lives. God is not responsible for the bad things that happen to us. Our own sin, the sin of others around us, and the sin of all those who came before us join together to produce a continuous shock wave of negative consequences in the world. God is not causing evil; he is trying, through the power of his Spirit, to restrain the evil that is so prevalent in the world.

God could erase sin at the snap of his fingers. In the blink of an eye, sin could be gone. And here is how he could do it. He could take away our freedom to choose. If we were unable to choose to go against God's will, there would be no sin, and we would be like a bunch of robots. But God did not do that because he loves us and desires that we be able to love him back—of our own free will.

What God does do is to cause all things, both good and bad, to work together for his ultimate glory and for our ultimate good. Look at the next phrase, "To work together for good." "Work together" is an interesting concept in the original language. Its literal meaning in the Greek has to do with weaving. Have you ever done needlepoint? I am an arts and crafts kind of guy, and I have tried my hand at it. My mother does great needlepoint. But if you look at the underside of her needlepoint, it is ugly. The thread on the underside of this artwork has all kinds of knots in it. There is thread, yarn, and string dangling everywhere.

If you were to just look at the underside of a piece of needlepoint, you would have very little appreciation for the beauty of the artwork. In fact, from your limited perspective, you would think it looks terrible. But if you turn it over, you see a completely different picture. All of those mangles and knots of thread on the underside work to create a tapestry of beauty that can only be seen from the top side of the fabric. From that vantage point, there is form to it, the colors come together, and it works visually in ways you would not have thought possible.

In life I often look at my problems and those of others close to me from just my limited perspective. I look underneath the problem, on the underside of the fabric, and nothing makes sense. I tell God that I just don't understand what he is trying to do with all of this disarray. How is God going to make something beautiful out of all the knots and dangling thread? But God has a plan, and he asks that I trust him to make something good out of the ugliness that I see. As I begin to see with the eyes of faith, he helps me lift my head up above the needlepoint, turn it around, and see what he is doing. When I begin to see the artwork from his perspective, through his eyes, then I begin to understand. I have faith that my life is beautiful in God's eyes, even though it might not always look that way to me now. It is a matter of perspective.

Can God take something evil and turn it into something good? You bet he can. Think of something as evil and horrible as the crucifixion of Jesus Christ. They took the sinless Son of God and tortured him. He hung there on the cross for our sins. God took something evil and made it into something wonderful for the salvation of the world. I have been pardoned and you have been pardoned through the death of Christ. Let's look at the remainder of the passage from Romans 8:28 (NASB): "God causes all things to work together for good to those who love God, to those who are called (remember this is just for Christians now) according to His purpose" (parenthetical comment added).

Even the trials, the evil things, the bad circumstances of life fulfill a greater purpose for "those who are called according to *His* purpose." While we suffer for a little while from sin and a fallen world, we long for the plans and purposes of God to be fulfilled. Our suffering loosens the grip the world has on our lives because it gives us a longing for heaven. If you have been called by God and saved by God, your life will ultimately be fulfilled by God in eternity. All that you have experienced—good, bad, and ugly—will come together in a beautiful tapestry. And finally you will be able to see what God sees as he looks down on the fine needlework in the fabric.

WE HAVE FREEDOM FROM OUR FEARS

The fourth reason why we should be the most hopeful persons is the premise of this entire book. Simply put, we have freedom from our fears. Psychologists have identified over 645 different fears or phobias, and they are still counting. I listed several of those phobias in the introduction to this book, and we have already dealt in some detail with the three greatest fears that we face.

Not surprisingly, the number one fear is the fear of death. People are afraid to die, to face that final chapter in their lives. We all have the desire to live because God gives us this desire. But eventually we are all going to die. And if you are outside of Christ, death should be something that you fear. The Bible says that one day we will face a holy and loving God. And he will ask us this question: Have you received my pardon? We will say either yes or no. My question to you right now is, Have you received Christ's pardon? If your answer is yes, there will be eternity in heaven for you. If it is no, you will face eternal separation from God. As Christians, we have nothing to fear about death.

The second greatest fear that we deal with is loneliness. I come in contact with so many lonely people. They have no real community at work, no real community in their neighborhood. They just don't know anyone in a real and authentic way. We all long for relationships because God has created us as relational beings. We cannot survive life on our own, as an island unto ourselves. We long for a personal relationship with Jesus Christ and for relationships with other human beings.

If you are in Christ, your relational base must be the church. The church has many ports of entry, many avenues where you can meet some life-changing friends. In the church you will find people who will surround you, love you, teach you, accept you, and forgive you. That is real community.

The third greatest fear is the fear of failure. We are fearful that if we step out, if we take a risk, if we try to challenge the unknown or conquer this obstacle or fulfill that dream, we might fail. I have met so many people over the course of my ministry who are terrified of taking a risk and trying something new. They rationalize to God, "I can't try that because I might fall flat on my face." That is why the Bible has such a real and vibrant message for our lives today. The Bible gives me example after example of men and women who have fallen flat on their faces. These are real, flesh-and-blood people who have messed up, some of them big time. They have taken a risk, stumbled and fallen, and yet God was able to pick up the pieces and use them in mighty ways.

I can identify with these ordinary men and women of the Bible. I fail all the time, and yet God still uses me. Jesus knows before it happens that we are going to fumble and fail and stumble and fall. He knows that, but he also tells us to get back up. He says, "I will forgive you. I will change you. I will work on you. And I will still use you." We should not fear failure because God makes his power known through imperfect vessels who are yielded to him in faith and obedience.

If you are outside of Christ, life can be scary. If you have not given your life to Christ, there is no one there to pick up the pieces. On the other hand, the Bible says this of those who are in Christ: "If God is for us, who can be against us?" (Rom. 8:31b). "Therefore, since we have such a hope, we are very bold" (2 Cor. 3:12). Do you realize that the Bible says "fear not" 365 times? That's one "fear not" for every day of the year. It is like God wanted that point to be obvious. So, fear not. If we are in Christ, we have freedom from our fears.

WE HAVE UNLIMITED RESOURCES

The fifth benefit of being a believer is that we have unlimited resources. I have a spiritual bank account that I can tap into that is phenomenal. Here is what the Word of God says: "Since he did not spare even his own Son for us but gave him up for us all" (Rom. 8:32 TLB). The essence of Christianity is giving, and God led the way by giving us Jesus Christ: "Won't he also surely give us everything else?" If God took care of our eternity by sending his best, what do we have to worry about? He will take care of all our needs.

Notice that God does not promise to meet our "greeds" but our needs. We have a tendency to mix up what we want out of selfishness and what we actually need. God knows better than we do what we need, and he will meet those needs. But he also knows what we *don't* need. He will often withhold things that we desire because he knows those things will become a distraction. Earthly treasures have a tendency to stand in the way of a deeper relationship with him.

It is amazing to me that many people who have been Christians for a long time are afraid to trust God with their abilities, talents, and finances. "Yeah, God, I will trust you for eternity. I have a ticket to heaven, but about using that gift I have in your church, about getting involved, about building a relationship, about giving money, at least 10 percent of what I make to you . . . no, God, I want to keep all of that for myself. You can have my eternity, but I will keep the rest for myself in the here and now."

God gives us the incomparable opportunity to contribute to his work in saving lives for eternity. We can express our thanks to him for what he has done in our lives by giving financially so the local church can continue to grow and thrive and impart to others the same hope we've been privileged to experience. We can multiply what we are doing exponentially to bring hope to a dying and fearful world. And if God has called you to a local church, he is tapping you on the shoulder and saying it is time to step up to the plate. It is time to test the waters of faith and dive deeper as you trust God with your finances.

Do you really trust God with everything? Every time the offering plate is passed, it is a matter of trust. You either trust him or you don't. If you trust him with eternity, maybe it's time to trust him with your finances as well.

Paul wrote to his younger brother in the Lord, Timothy, in 1 Timothy 6:17, "Command those who are rich in this present world." We are all rich. Every single person reading these words is rich. If you had the money to buy this book, you are rich. If you have more than one outfit to wear, you are rich, compared to the world's standards. I believe American Christians in particular are rich in relation to the varying degrees of wealth in the world today.

Paul continued, "Not to be arrogant nor to put their hope in wealth, which is so uncertain." Wouldn't you agree with that? Wealth is uncertain. If you don't believe this, talk to some people who lived through the early 1980s when fortunes made in oil and real estate collapsed. They will tell you that worldly wealth is uncertain. Ask some of the people in the last several years who put their financial hopes in technology stocks, only to have the bottom drop out of the tech sector. The passage concludes, "But to put their hope in God, who richly provides us with everything for our enjoyment."

God wants us to have a blast here on this earth, a life of adventure. Faith is the precursor to hope, and we have talked about faith quite a bit over the course of this book. A good description of a life of faith is adventure and excitement. He wants that life for you. Trust him with every aspect of your life. Don't hold back in any area, and you will be able to tap into the unlimited resources of an adventurous and exciting life of faith.

WE HAVE ETERNAL SECURITY

The sixth benefit of being a believer has to do with our eternal destiny. I have security forever through the person of Jesus Christ, who embodies the final hope of the believer. Paul assures us in Romans 8:38–39, "For I am convinced that neither death nor life, neither angels nor demons, neither the present nor the future." All of us have a longing for eternity. We saw earlier in Ecclesiastes that the desire for eternity has been placed in our hearts. Have you ever wondered why most little children's books end with "and they lived happily ever after"? We have this desire for a happy ending. When we go see a movie and it has a bad ending, we don't like the movie because the ending leaves a bad taste in our mouths. God has set eternity in our hearts, and an unhappy ending does not compute with what we know in our hearts is supposed to happen.

Have you ever been reading a novel, and it gets so exciting that you have to flip to the last chapter to see the ending in order to relieve the tension? I did that recently. I just couldn't take the suspense. If we are in Christ, we have read the last chapter. God has already revealed the final page. And we win. We spend eternity with Jesus. We must come to a moment of decision in our lives when we say, "Jesus Christ, I admit to you I am on death row. I deserve eternal separation, but I realize now that I have been pardoned. And I accept your pardon." When we do that, we are born again into the family of God, and our eternity is secure.

It is like when I hold the hand of my twins, Laurie and Landra, as we are walking across a busy intersection. If they try to let go, I won't let them because I am their father. I have grasped their hand to deliver them safely to the other side, and nothing could loosen my grip on my daughters' hands. The twins can wiggle and squirm and try to pull away, but my grip is secure. The moment you clasp your hand with God, the moment you do that through Jesus Christ, he will not let go. You might wiggle and squirm from time to time and even spend part of your Christian life in rebellion, trying to pull away, but he will not let go. This a forever deal: "Neither angels nor demons, neither the present nor the future, nor any powers, neither height nor depth, nor anything else in all creation, will be able to separate us from the love of God that is in Christ Jesus our Lord."

Whenever I think about heaven, I wonder why God has not told us more in the Bible about this incredible place where we will spend eternity. I think if the Bible told us more about heaven and how great it's going to be, we would be doing irrational things to get there in a hurry. We have taken a hard look at the afterlife in a previous chapter, and we know about the incredible future that awaits the believer in Christ. We have discovered together that heaven is a perfect place, and it is a place where our gifts and abilities can be showcased and used to the maximum. It will be an adventure that will build and build in intensity throughout eternity. It will be awesome.

I am reminded of C. S. Lewis's imagery of heaven in his concluding book of the Chronicles of Narnia, *The Last Battle*. As the world of Narnia draws to an end, those who belong to the great lion, Aslan, are drawn out of the "shadowlands" of the old, dying Narnia and into the final reality of their new, eternal home. As they go "further in and further up" into this new world, which resembles the old Land of Narnia, the authenticity, beauty, and size of the heavenly landscape increases continually. Like ever-expanding concentric circles, the glory and majesty of the great beyond grows and builds forever.

While Lewis's work is fictional and only an imagining of things to come, it is a compelling description of the unimaginable beauty and continual adventure we will experience in heaven. We will spend infinitely more time in heaven or in eternity than we spend in this life. And what we do down here influences what will happen there.

Are you in Christ? If you are, do you realize the benefits of a believer? Are those benefits making a difference in how you live your life and interact with others on a daily basis?

So What?

Let me ask you a two-word question: So what? You have seen the reasons for hope. You know that hope is a person, Jesus Christ, and you have no reason to fear if you are in Christ. You have read about the benefits of the Christian life as a result of the hope that we have through Christ. But so what? Let me give you a couple of things to do that will help you apply these principles in your daily life.

First, be prepared to share your hope with others. The Book of 1 Peter says it like this: "But in your hearts set apart Christ as Lord. Always be prepared to give an answer to everyone who asks you to give the reason for the hope that you have. But do this with gentleness and respect" (1 Pet. 3:15). If your life reflects the benefits of being a believer, people will ask you, "Why are you that way? Why do you have joy? Why do you have confidence, even when it is tough for you, even when you have just lost a loved one or broken off a relationship? Why do you have this peace in the midst of your tears? How do you do it?" The world will give you a window to share what you believe.

Have you ever shared sparks of Jesus Christ with others? Sadly, the world today is more prepared to receive this message than many of us are to give it. Are you reflecting confidence and hope in every area of your life? People are watching. They are checking you out.

Second, copy the "Facing Life's Phobias" section at the end of this chapter on a card and put that card in a prominent place in your house, maybe on the bathroom mirror, in your Bible, or on the bedside table. If you are like me, you sometimes feel down and even whine and complain. We need to wake up and say, "Wait a minute." We can say, "Look who I am in Christ." Go through these benefits, memorize them, and understand who you are in Christ. Then people will be able to see these benefits reflected in your life and will want some of what you have.

It is a little like an aquarium my family has at home. This aquarium has a couple of fish and a little freshwater shrimp named Jason. We throw fish food into the aquarium, and the minnows are quick to eat it. But the little freshwater shrimp Jason is kind of slow. He doesn't have fins, and he just kicks himself along the bottom. He waits for the food to drift down. When it gets down on his level, he grabs it with his long shrimplike fingers and eats it. And here is something that I could not believe when I first saw it. The shrimp is translucent. If he eats red food, he turns red. You can actually see it pass through his stomach.

If we feed on the Word of God, if we feed on the benefits of being a believer, if we know who we are in Christ, the world can look at us and see all the spiritual food we've been digesting. They will see our joy and hope because we are translucent in a sense. What are you feeding on, the world's garbage or the bread of life? If you are prepared to share the hope you have with others and are meditating daily on the benefits of believing in God's Word, you will know the mystery that has been revealed in Christ—a hope that never fails.

Facing Life's Phobias

I HAVE BEEN PARDONED

- To them God has chosen to make known among the Gentiles the glorious riches of this mystery, which is Christ in you, the hope of glory (Col. 1:27).
- So there is now no condemnation awaiting those who belong to Christ Jesus (Rom. 8:1 TLB).
- But now we have a far better hope, for Christ makes us acceptable to God, and now we may draw near to him (Heb. 7:19b TLB).

I HAVE THE POWER TO CHANGE

- For the power of the life-giving Spirit—and this power is mine through Christ Jesus—has freed me from the vicious circle of sin and death (Rom. 8:2 TLB).
- And we know that God causes all things to work together for good to those who love God, to those who are called according to His purpose (Rom. 8:28 NASB).

I Have Freedom from My Fears

- If God is for us, who can be against us? (Rom. 8:31b).
- Therefore, since we have such a hope, we are very bold (2 Cor. 3:12).

I Have Unlimited Resources

- Since he did not spare even his own Son for us but gave him up for us all, won't he also surely give us everything else? (Rom. 8:32 TLB).
- Command those who are rich in this present world not to be arrogant nor to put their hope in wealth, which is so uncertain, but to put their hope in God, who richly provides us with everything for our enjoyment (1 Tim. 6:17).

I Have Eternal Security

- For I am convinced that neither death nor life, neither angels nor demons, neither the present nor the future, nor any powers, neither height nor depth, nor anything else in all creation, will be able to separate us from the love of God that is in Christ Jesus our Lord (Rom. 8:38–39).

So What?

- But in your hearts set apart Christ as Lord. Always be prepared to give an answer to everyone who asks you to give the reason for the hope that you have. But do this with gentleness and respect (1 Pet. 3:15).

THE FINAL WORD

And the Greatest of These

It is amazing how many classes and courses are being offered these days. You can take Tae Kwon Do classes, sushi-making classes, mountain-climbing classes, or snowboarding classes. A friend of mine told me recently that he is enrolled in calf-roping lessons. I am thinking about taking a fly-fishing course. Although classes and courses are interesting, we could miss a couple of the ones I just named, and it wouldn't change the trajectory of our lives. Rarely are classes offered on the most important dimensions of our lives: classes on marriage, dating, parenting, or even on this chapter's subject matter—love.

I have never had a person walk up to me in tears and look me in the eye and say, "Ed, I need prayer because my sushi rolls are falling apart." "I need counseling because I can't seem to get the knack of snowboarding." I don't get those statements. But I do get a steady stream of letters and calls from people whose lives are messed up relationally, emotionally, and spiritually because they are ignorant of, or have not taken to heart, the kind of subject matter that really

chapter 10

matters. I am talking about the eternal truth found in the Word of God.

In this concluding chapter, we will take a crash course in the greatest subject in all the world—love. Love is the final word on fear. We have already seen from our study on the fear of God that "perfect love drives out fear" (1 John 4:18). So it is fitting, I believe, to end this book on fear with an in-depth look at biblical love. It is tempting for me to begin this discussion by jumping right into the facets of love and giving you practical, everyday applications of love. We will do that in a little while. But if we are to understand how to give and experience true love, we first must grasp God's love for us.

LOVE IN ACTION

There is a lot of confusion about love going around these days. Some people confuse love with an emotion. They say that love is a feeling. Tina Turner called it a secondhand emotion. I hate to say this to Tina, but love is not a feeling. Love is not an emotion. It causes feelings and it causes emotions, but it is neither a feeling nor an emotion. God commands us to love him and others, but he does not command feelings. Feelings cannot be commanded or demanded. As an earthly father I can't say to my children, "Kids, I command you to be happy." They would probably reply, "We're trying. We're trying to be happy, Daddy." But, if they do not feel happy, all the trying in the world is not going to make them have feelings of happiness. Love is much more than a feeling or an emotion.

Other people confuse love with lust. Love is not lust. Lust cannot wait to get, but love cannot wait to give. And for many people these days love is pseudo-love, or thinly veiled selfishness. We like to make this magnanimous statement: "I love you." But if you read the fine print, a person may actually be saying, "I'll love you if you meet my needs, if you are sweet to me, if you are kind, if you show me affection. But the moment you stop doing that I won't love you any more."

People talk about falling in love like you fall into a swimming pool. And popular culture feeds this idea just about everywhere you turn. But love, according to the author of love, is a decision. The Bible explodes all of this confusion and nails it down precisely in 1 John 3:18 (TLB): "Little children, let us stop just saying we love people; let us really love them, and show it by our actions." Love is a choice, and it always reveals itself in action.

Here is what God wants to do in our lives. God loves us so much that he wants to take us from the natural realm of loving into the supernatural realm of loving. God wants to do that and he will do it if we can answer two important questions about love and incorporate these answers into our lives. We will spend the lion's share of this last chapter addressing these two questions.

HOW DOES GOD EXPRESS HIS LOVE FOR ME?

The first question is: How does God express his love for me? Bill Hybels in his book *Seven Wonders of the Spiritual World,* uses the analogy of human relationships as a contrast to God's unfathomable love for us. He begins by writing, "It is no small thing to say to another human being, 'I love you.'"[1] That is a high-risk pronouncement. If you are married, think back to the time you were dating. For some it might be a longer jaunt down memory lane than for others. Do you remember those "statements at the door," guys? You

231

walk her to the door and after the first or maybe second date you take the risk and say, "I really had a nice time tonight." And you are hoping and praying that she returns the sentiment by saying, "I had a nice time too." And if you get past that hurdle you think, *Oh boy, I'm cruising now.*

A couple of weeks later, you face the next hurdle. You begin to get a little more vulnerable and say something like, "I really enjoy being with you." You wait anxiously, and she hopefully says it back. Then you walk to your car and shout, "Yes." But at this point you are putting off the inevitable. You are starting to realize that you love her and know it is just a matter of time before you will have to say that three-word sentence, that high-risk pronouncement.

The next time you see her, your palms are sweaty and your heart is racing. You look into her eyes and begin to work up to it: "Of all the girls I have dated, you are the most special. You are incredible." Then, finally, you know you have to say it. You think to yourself that if you say it and she rejects it, you will be devastated. But finally you realize that you must be real. You must be true to your feelings. You must take the risk. You come to that point when you look into her eyes and say, "I love you." You've unloaded the tremendous weight from your chest, the cards are on the table, you have shown your hand, and you have taken the mystery out of the relationship. And then, to your great relief and delight, she responds to your bold pronouncement by saying, "I love you too."

God makes this high-risk pronouncement right out of the gate. He doesn't have to work up to it or wait for the right cues from us before he takes the risk. God comes right out and says it. Even though he knows we might reject it, even though he knows we might spurn it, even though he knows we might turn our backs on it, God says it over and over again: "I love you. I love you. I love you." And when you make a statement like that, you have to back it up because love costs something. God didn't just stop with saying, "I love you." He actually put it in print, in bold print. He went on record in the Book, the Bible.

He writes it down. The first way that God expresses his love to us is through documentation. He has written it down. And God has written it down over and over again so people will never waver on the point and not have to wonder or speculate. He writes things like this to us: In Isaiah 43:1 (NASB), he says, "Do not fear, for I have redeemed you; I have called you by name; you are Mine!" In Romans 5:8 (NASB), he declares, "God demonstrates His own love toward us, in that while we were yet sinners, Christ died for us." And in Jeremiah 31:3, he says, "The LORD appeared to us in the past, saying: 'I have loved you with an everlasting love; I have drawn you with loving-kindness.'" God assures us repeatedly that his love will never run out. Don't ever confuse his love with human love.

I have talked over the years to many people who tell me they have committed a sin that has broken the back of God's love. People really believe they can bankrupt the love of God. And I love to point them to this passage: "I have loved you with an everlasting love." The Bible says that God *is* love, so he cannot walk away from love any more than he can walk away from himself. His very nature reaches out to us and extends love and forgiveness, no matter how bad we've blown it, no matter what we think we've done that would cause him to stop loving us.

We are talking about love in a supernatural realm. We can't possibly completely comprehend the depths of God's love because our finite minds are incapable of calculating God's infinite character qualities. But, while God has a kind of love that we cannot comprehend, we can receive it and count on it as much as we count on God himself.

He illustrates it. God also expresses his love for us through illustration. One of my favorite magazines is *Sports Illustrated.* My brother Ben and I would take every issue of *SI* and remove the cover and a variety of article illustrations ranging from badminton to boxing, volleyball to football, and we would save them. We then made a sports collage in our room. Our walls and ceiling were covered with sports pictures. During the 70s a collage was the thing to do. You could walk into our bedroom and no matter what sport you were into, you could find some sort of picture to connect with. In essence, God has given us, through the pages of Scripture, a love collage. As we walk into God's room, he knows that certain ones of us will connect with certain word pictures. He uses a great variety of word pictures to communicate, express, and illustrate his love to us.

I presented a series of messages several years ago called "Animal Planet," in which I talked about how God uses various animals throughout the Bible to illustrate different truths. In Matthew 23:37, for example, God says, "How often I have longed to gather your children together, as a hen gathers her chicks under her wings." God talks about his love in Proverbs by comparing it to the love a lioness or a bear has for her cubs. If you are a scientist, God says in Psalm 103:11 (NASB), "For as high as the heavens are above the earth, so great is His lovingkindness toward those who fear Him."

Maybe you are able to make a better connection with the parental picture of God's love. If you are a mother, Isaiah 49:15 can be that word picture for you: "Can a mother forget the baby at her breast and have no compassion on the child she has borne? Though she may forget, I will not forget you!" If you are a father, Psalm 103:13 may be for you: "As a father has compassion on his children, so the LORD has compassion on those who fear him."

If you have a best friend who means a lot to you, you might connect with a picture of the love one friend has for another. Christ says in John 15:13, "Greater love has no one than this, that he lay down his life for his friends." Or if you are an athlete who is familiar with the concept of discipline, read passages like 2 Timothy 1:7: "For God did not give us a spirit of timidity, but a spirit of power, of love and of self-discipline." God uses a great variety of illustrations and descriptions to bring home to each of us a word picture of his great love for us.

He demonstrates it. It is great that God has told me this, but how does he show it? How does God really reveal his love for us? How does he express it? Remember, God expresses it in print—that is, through documentation. God expresses it in word pictures—that is, by way of illustration. Most significantly, though, God also expresses his love in practice. God's love is not just a bunch of rhetoric or a nice little story to make us feel warm and fuzzy. God has taken his love to the mat. He has shown us his love in many tangible ways. He has truly demonstrated his love to humanity.

Take a quick glance through history. God demonstrated his love to Adam and Eve. After they sinned, he gave them a second chance. Look at Noah and his family. They were about to get into some serious flooding problems, and God delivered them and saved them because of his love. Abraham was going to sacrifice his son Isaac, and God demonstrated his love to Abraham by providing a ram in place of his son. When David committed adultery with Bathsheba, God demonstrated his love to David by forgiving him.

You could go on and on throughout the pages of Scripture until you come to God's ultimate demonstration of his love in the person and work of Jesus. God expressed his love in the most profound way possible by sending Jesus Christ. He left his home in heaven, put on flesh, humbled himself to the place of suffering, and got knocked around on the playing field of life. God offered Jesus Christ, his only and precious Son, as a sin sacrifice for nondeserving people like us. And the cross stands as the ultimate symbol of God's love.

One of the most-quoted passages in all the Bible says it best: "For God so loved the world, that He gave His only begotten Son, that whoever believes in Him should not perish, but have eternal life" (John 3:16 NASB).

But it doesn't end there because God gets specific. God tells us throughout the pages of Scripture, "I have loved you since you were born. I have reached out to you. I have offered you guidance. I have offered you salvation. I have offered you a home in heaven. You are mine, and my love is right there for you. You either receive it or you don't."

We do one of two things with God's love: We either receive God's love, or we reject God's love. It is as simple as that. For those of us who receive God's love, we open up our hearts and discover a love so wide, high, and deep that it is only natural for us to want to return God's love by giving of our time, abilities, talents, and treasures. It is a natural thing to love God and to want to express our feelings of love and gratitude toward him.

But many people have rejected God's love. They have turned their backs on it, have explained it away, have put it off. And they may even be saying to themselves, "Some day, I will get right with God." God also says there will be a some day, and that some day is called a day of reckoning.

Many people will face God on that day of reckoning. God will look into their eyes and say, "I have loved you since you were born. I have provided a way for you. I have protected you from Satan's attacks in areas that you will never even know about. I have offered my love to you through that relationship, through that message, through that drama, through that Bible study, through that friend, but you kept on rejecting my love. You kept on saying you wanted to do it your way." And in essence, God will say on that day, "You had your way on earth, and now you will have your way in eternity. You will spend eternity apart from me in hell."

We choose heaven or hell. God doesn't force it on us. He has offered the opportunity for everyone to spend eternity with him, but some people reject God's love. God expresses his love to us. He has put it in writing. He has illustrated it. And he has demonstrated it. I will ask again the question that I have been asking throughout this book: Have you received it?[2]

HOW DO I EXPRESS GOD'S LOVE TO OTHERS?

Let's jump to the next important question about love. If I am in contact with God's love, how do I express this love to others? I have this love that is so phenomenal. I have discovered it. I have accepted it. I am returning it to God. How do I express it to others?

Service. The Bible says that we express God's love to others by serving them. Love and service are inseparably linked. The Bible says that all of us have unique abilities and talents. I am not going to differentiate between spiritual and natural gifts because God gives them all to us to be used for his glory and in service to others. If you are hooked up with a local church, you see these gifts and talents played out on a weekly basis. You see people with the gift of teaching every time you hear a life-changing message or participate in a Bible study or class. You see others with artistic abilities, perhaps in multimedia or music or drama.

For example, God has gifted a drummer with the talent to play drums. God has given him rhythm. Did God give him rhythm just for himself? Did God want the drummer to spend eternity in a little shell just playing away for himself and his own pleasure? How about those with vocal talent? God has gifted these people with the ability to sing. Does God want singers to stand in a little soundproof room for the rest of their lives and into eternity and just sing for themselves? God has blessed us with gifts. He wants us to bless others by using our gifts, by serving others, and by getting involved in people's lives.

Christians talk a lot about serving God. "Service" is one of the spiritual buzzwords in the church. And many people in the church are actually doing it in various ministries within the church. You may be involved in your church in the preschool ministry, the children's ministry, sound and lighting, drama, video, or a small-group ministry. You are putting action behind your words. You are serving others. On a more practical level, though, are you serving the people closest to you on a daily basis? Are you serving your spouse? Are you serving your children? Are you serving the people you work with and work for? Do you have an attitude of service twenty-four hours a day and seven days a week?

Jesus articulated one of the great ironies of spiritual greatness in Mark 9:35: "If anyone wants to be first, he must be the very last, and the servant of all." If you want to be great, you must become a servant. So I am going to give you an assignment to bring this curriculum on love home to you on a practical level. For the next seven days do one act of service secretly each day for one person or seven different persons.

You may choose your spouse as the recipient of your "secret service." Or you may have seven children (God bless you!) and choose to perform an act of service for each one over the next seven days. You may work with several individuals in your office, but there is one person in particular who really needs to know that somebody loves him or her. Show the love of Christ to that person this week by serving him or her.

Recently, I decided to clean the kitchen. I told Lisa to relax and that I would take care of the kids and clean up the kitchen. As I cleaned the kitchen, I began to sing a little song: "He is a servant. Ed is a servant. Watch Ed serve. Watch him clean." That is drawing attention to yourself. I am talking about service without pointing to yourself to get the credit. It is secret service in the most fundamental and spiritual sense.

Commitment. Love should also express itself through commitment. We must be committed. Love and commitment, like love and service, go hand in hand. How many people these days say they have decided just to live together so they can test the waters. And then maybe later, if their trial run works out, they will get married. This is not love. This is affection. Love is commitment. It is not afraid of the risk. Love says to the other person, "I am going to hang in there even though I don't feel like it all the time, even though the emotions don't always gel together. I am committed to you."

The same thing is true in your commitment to the other people in your life, your work, your friendships, and your church. When was the last time you verbalized your commitment to a friend or coworker, someone special to you, someone you are with daily?

When was the last time you committed to a local body of Christ? Many people show up at church every week and get fed from the Word of God, but they are eating free, living off the rest of us who give of our time, talents, and treasures. Maybe it is time for you to make a commitment to be a part of a local body of believers—I mean a real commitment. The Bible commands us to be a part of the local body of Christ: "Let us not give up meeting together, as some are in the habit of doing, but let us encourage one another— and all the more as you see the Day approaching" (Heb. 10:25).

There are several good reasons to make a commitment to the church, not the least of which is a biblical reason: Christ is committed to his church, and he wants the same from us. There is also a cultural reason: the church has the antidote for the deep moral problems that plague our society. And then we have a practical reason for the pragmatists out there: commitment defines in a quantitative sense who can be counted on to serve and carry out the many functions within the church. Are you committed? Or are you still riding the fence, keeping your options open, waiting for something better to come along? You'll never experience anything better than being committed with all of your strength, passion, and resources to the body of Christ.

As the pastor of a large church, I receive many letters. But I received some letters recently that really stirred my heart about the impact that Fellowship Church has had on several people's lives. The first one reads, "We have never experienced such a loving and generous church family anywhere. We were lost until we found the Fellowship. I don't know what my life would be like without this church. The people really care about us as Christians and as individuals."

Another person writes, "My husband and I accepted Christ as the result of attending [Fellowship]. Christ healed our broken marriage and blessed us with a beautiful, healthy girl. We were blessed with a wonderful home team of believers who genuinely care about our lives."

Another letter reads, "We were on the verge of divorce. Since coming to the Fellowship, we truly have learned and experienced what love and commitment is. With God in our lives, we will be able to make it."

These letters represent just a small sampling of what can happen when people give themselves in love, service, and commitment to the church. People's lives hang in the balance, and we in the church have the lifeline. My hat goes off to those who are committed to a personal relationship with the Lord, to the family, and to service in the church.

Sacrifice. Another way we express love is through sacrifice. Sacrifice means to give the best we have for a better purpose. Are you living out sacrificial love? Are you giving the best you have for a greater purpose? Are you giving the best, even though someone will not pat you on the back, even though it is really going to cost you something? People often wonder how to cure materialism in the lives of their children. One of the ways you do it is by giving and sacrificing the best you have so you can model to your children the principle that things are not as important as your personal relationship with the living Lord and your commitment to his church. The Bible calls this kind of sacrifice our "first fruits," the first and best part of what we have.

It hurts to give sacrificially. That is the point of the exercise of sacrificial giving. When we give sacrificially, it communicates to God and others our priorities in life. We are giving up certain things that are less important in order to contribute to and build up things that are more important. Paul described the gifts he received from the Philippian church to support his ministry as an "acceptable sacrifice" in Philippians 4:18: "I have received from Epaphroditus the gifts you sent. They are a fragrant offering, an acceptable sacrifice, pleasing to God."

Are you giving sacrificially to the work of God through the local church? Many people have decided to put some purchases on hold, have decided that they don't need to own certain things, have decided to spend less on Christmas gift giving so they can give sacrificially to the eternal work of the church. And that kind of sacrificial giving is making a lasting impression on the lives of our children. Sacrificial love is one of the cornerstones of the Christian life.

Sharing. Another way we express love is by sharing the faith and hope we have with others. One of the most loving things you can do is share the Lord Jesus Christ with others. Invite them to church with you. Share with them what the Lord has done in your life. Love gives us no other option. Paul says that the love of Christ "compels us" (2 Cor. 5:14) to share the gospel of Christ with others and to help bring reconciliation between them and God. We must be committed to what Christ was committed to, and Christ was committed to people. He loved people, and he said that we are to be committed to and love people. Are you loving people? Are you sharing the bread of life with people? Are you shining the light of God's truth in a dark and fearful world?

Jesus said in the Sermon on the Mount that we cannot hide the light that is in us any more than a city set on a hill can be hidden. "You are the light of the world. A city on a hill cannot be hidden. Neither do people light a lamp and put it under a bowl. Instead they put it on its stand, and it gives light to everyone in the house. In the same way, let your light shine before men, that they may see your good deeds and praise your Father in heaven" (Matt. 5:14–16).

The light of God's truth is meant to shine in the darkness, not to be hidden within the four walls of the church building. The bread of life is meant to be shared with others so they can come to the light and experience the love of God.

We come now to the classic text on love and the final word on fear. You've heard it many times, at weddings, in sermons, and in songs. First Corinthians 13:13 says, "These three remain: faith, hope, and love. But the greatest of these is love." I have to admit that this text puzzled me for a long time. Why does the Bible say that the greatest of the three is love? We have taken a look throughout this book at the various ways that faith, hope, and love are antidotes to our earthly fears. But why is love the greatest?

Here is why, I believe, that love is the greatest of the three. Once we get to heaven we won't need any more faith because we will see the Lord, the object of our faith, face-to-face. As for hope, who needs hope once everything we have hoped for is finally realized? Every need is met, every fear is vanquished, and every dream is realized to the tenth power and beyond. The only thing that will remain is love, a love that never leaves because God himself is the ultimate embodiment of pure love. Love is the final word on fear because God's perfect love, which casts out all fear, sustains us now and forever.

Facing Life's Phobias

LOVE IN ACTION

- "Little children, let us stop just saying we love people; let us really love them, and show it by our actions" (1 John 3:18 TLB).

HOW DOES GOD EXPRESS HIS LOVE FOR ME?

- *He writes it down.* "Do not fear, for I have redeemed you; I have called you by name; you are Mine!" (Isa. 43:1 NASB). But God demonstrates His own love toward us, in that while we were yet sinners, Christ died for us (Rom. 5:8 NASB). The

LORD appeared to us in the past, saying, "I have loved you with an everlasting love; I have drawn you with loving-kindness" (Jer. 31:3).

- *He illustrates it.* "How often I have longed to gather your children together, as a hen gathers her chicks under her wings" (Matt. 23:37). For as high as the heavens are above the earth, so great is His lovingkindness toward those who fear Him (Ps. 103:11 NASB). "Can a mother forget the baby at her breast and have no compassion on the child she has borne? Though she may forget, I will not forget you!" (Isa. 49:15). As a father has compassion on his children, so the LORD has compassion on those who fear him (Ps. 103:13). "Greater love has no one than this, that he lay down his life for his friends" (John 15:13). For God did not give us a spirit of timidity, but a spirit of power, of love and of self-discipline (2 Tim. 1:7).

- *He demonstrates it.* "For God so loved the world, that He gave His only begotten Son, that whoever believes in Him should not perish, but have eternal life" (John 3:16 NASB).

HOW DO I EXPRESS GOD'S LOVE TO OTHERS?

- *Service.* "If anyone wants to be first, he must be the very last, and the servant of all" (Mark 9:35).

- *Commitment.* Let us not give up meeting together, as some are in the habit of doing, but let us encourage one another—and all the more as you see the Day approaching (Heb. 10:25).

- *Sacrifice.* I have received from Epaphroditus the gifts you sent. They are a fragrant offering, an acceptable sacrifice, pleasing to God (Phil. 4:18).

- *Sharing.* For Christ's love compels us, because we are convinced that one died for all, and therefore all died (2 Cor. 5:14). "You are the light of the world. A city on a hill cannot be hidden. Neither do people light a lamp and put it under a bowl. Instead they put it on its stand, and it gives light to everyone in the house. In the same way, let your light shine before men, that they may see your good deeds and praise your Father in heaven" (Matt. 5:14–16).

THE FINAL WORD

- "These three remain: faith, hope and love. But the greatest of these is love" (1 Cor. 13:13).

NOTES

INTRODUCTION

1. www.mille.org.
2. www.isd.net/grezac/html/Phobias/byphob.htm.

CHAPTER 1

1. Dan Rather, *CBS News,* 18 October 2001.
2. Rick Hampson, "Terror Tactics Rarely Triumph," *USA Today,* 1 November 2001.
3. Nanci Hellmich and Robert Davis, *USA Today,* 16 October 2001.
4. George Will, "Now, Weapons of Mass Disruption?" *Newsweek,* 29 October 2001.
5. Fox News Network, *Fox News Live,* 18 December 2001.
6. Ernest Becker, *The Denial of Death* (New York: Free Press, 1997).

CHAPTER 3

1. Ed Young, *The Ulti-Mate* (HeartSprings Media, 2000), 58–61. (In addition to *The Ulti-Mate,* I recommend *The One,* cowritten by my brother Ben Young and Dr. Samuel Adams. Both books are available on-line at fellowshipchurch.com.)

CHAPTER 4

1. *Nelson's New Illustrated Bible Dictionary,* Electronic edition, Logos Library System (Nashville: Thomas Nelson, 1997).

CHAPTER 5

1. Larry Crabb, *Understanding Who You Are* (Colorado Springs: NavPress, 1997), 5.

CHAPTER 6

1. www.longtolive.com.
2. C. S. Lewis, *The Great Divorce* (New York: Macmillan Publishing Company, 1946), 19.
3. George W. Robinson, "I Am His and He Is Mine."

CHAPTER 7

1. Philip Yancey, *Soul Survivor* (New York: Doubleday, 2001), 207.
2. Ibid, 213.
3. Ibid, 214.

CHAPTER 8

1. *Nelson's New Illustrated Bible Commentary* (Nashville: Thomas Nelson, 1997).

CHAPTER 10

1. Bill Hybels, *Seven Wonders of the Spiritual World* (Word, 1988), 42.
2. I owe a debt of gratitude to Bill Hybels for his insights into God's love. His work, *Seven Wonders of the Spiritual World,* has spurred my thinking throughout this section.